In Business

Teacher's book

Graham White and
Margaret Khidhayir

Nelson

Thomas Nelson and Sons Ltd
Nelson House   Mayfield Road
Walton-on-Thames   Surrey
KT12 5PL   UK

51 York Place
Edinburgh
EH1 3JD   UK

Thomas Nelson (Hong Kong) Ltd
Toppan Building 10/F
22A Westland Road
Quarry Bay   Hong Kong

Thomas Nelson Australia
480 La Trobe Street
Melbourne   Victoria 3000
Australia

Nelson Canada
1120 Birchmount Road
Scarborough   Ontario
M1K 5G4   Canada

© Topaz Projects Ltd, 1983

First published by George G. Harrap and Co. Ltd., 1983
ISBN 0-245-53804-6

This edition published by Thomas Nelson and Sons Ltd 1990
ISBN 0-17-444193-2
NPN 9 8 7 6

All rights reserved. No paragraph of this publication may be reproduced, copied or transmitted save with written permission or in accordance with the provisions of the Copyright, Design and Patents Act 1988, or under the terms of any licence permitting limited copying issued by the Copyright Licensing Agency, 33-34 Alfred Place, London WC1E 7DP.

Any person who does any unauthorised act in relation to this publication may be liable to criminal prosecution and civil claims for damages.

Printed in Hong Kong

Contents

Introduction　　　　　　　　　　　5
　Format
　Themes
　Analysis of language
　Methodology

Syllabus　　　　　　　　　　　　7

Unit-by-unit guide　　　　　　　11
　1　The Executives' Conference (1)　　11
　2　The Executives' Conference (2)　　15
　3　More or less　　　　　　　　　　18
　4　All shapes and sizes　　　　　　　21
　5　Disaster at Swinton Road　　　　24
　6　Facts and figures　　　　　　　　26
　7　Here's how　　　　　　　　　　28
　8　No sooner said than done!　　　　30
　9　Consolidation exercises　　　　　32
　10　Plans, arrangements and decisions　34
　11　Go West, young man!　　　　　36
　12　What do you think?　　　　　　38
　13　The customer is always right　　　40
　14　A new appointment　　　　　　42
　15　What would you suggest?　　　　45
　16　Weighing it up　　　　　　　　47
　17　Better than ever　　　　　　　　49
　18　Consolidation exercises　　　　　52
　19　Expanding overseas　　　　　　54
　20　Business abroad　　　　　　　　57
　21　That's what must have happened　59
　22　The new production plant　　　　62
　23　Could I have your views?　　　　64
　24　Tell me why　　　　　　　　　66
　25　That's the way it is　　　　　　68
　26　Keep the customer satisfied　　　70
　27　Consolidation exercises　　　　　72

Introduction

In Business is intended for adult students of business English who have already reached intermediate level. It aims to provide students with the practical language skills needed to communicate effectively in a wide range of business situations.

Format

The full course contains 24 programme units (each containing up to 12 steps) and three consolidation units (Units 9, 18 and 27). In each programme unit there are listening and reading exercises, controlled language practice, laboratory drills, writing exercises, role play and decision-making activities. The consolidation units contain exercises on the language presented in the previous eight units.

Listening texts and laboratory drills are recorded on cassettes (or tapes) and are numbered (tape section 1 to tape section 67) for ease of reference. The laboratory drills are printed in full in the Teacher's Book as they occur. All other tapescripts are printed in the Student's Book, always near the end of the unit in which they occur.

The following symbols are used throughout the Student's Book and Teacher's Book to indicate the main activity of a step:

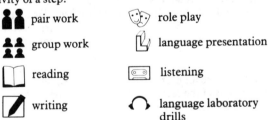

Themes

The units centre on the fortunes of two subsidiaries of a Swiss multinational called UMC. The subsidiaries are *Ambermold International*, UK-based manufacturers of roller bearings, and *The Fittenwell Group*, a Swiss pharmaceutical company. Themes include conferences, job interviews, placing orders, insurance, statistics, business meetings, complaints, presentation techniques, investment, technical specifications, overseas

representation and production. There is no storyline; thematically each unit is self-contained.

Analysis of language

The authors have not rigidly adhered to one particular analysis of language in their selection of exponents to be presented.

For example, Units 5 and 10 teach grammatical structures, Units 2 and 20 deal with the linguistic realization of specific language functions, Unit 4 deals with the notions of number and dimension.

Methodology

The authors have tried to move away from the traditional pattern of the EFL textbook unit, i.e.:

Presentation of Language → *Controlled Practice* → *Free Stage*

Instead, they have preferred to add an extra stage at the beginning:

1 *Language Activity* → 2 *Extraction of Language* → 3 *Controlled Practice* → 4 *Free Stage*

There are two reasons for this.
1 To ensure that new language is encountered in context (communicative purpose).
2 To establish a need for a particular area of language (diagnostic purpose).

Having established that need, the authors go on to present paradigms of language (*Extraction of Language*), provide opportunities for learning these forms through written exercises and in the language laboratory (*Controlled Practice*), and finally set up a situation in which students use all the language at their disposal to solve a problem (*Free Stage*).

Message and language

Stages 1 and 4 focus on *message*, stages 2 and 3 focus on *language*. The language input is more difficult at stages 1 and 4; the authors feel it is important that students learn to deal with language which they cannot yet produce, but have tried to help the student by simplifying the listening and reading tasks he or she is asked to perform. The teacher should aim at successful completion of the task and not attempt to explain every word of the text. On the other hand, teachers should insist on accuracy at stage 3, when discrete items of language are being practised in controlled situations.

To exemplify this four-stage pattern, Unit 1 step 1 contains a note-taking and reading activity on the theme of company structure. In step 2 students concentrate on the information they have extracted during note-taking and, after presentation and practice of appropriate question forms, exchange information in pairs. This controlled practice of question forms, based on information provided, is followed by a free stage practice in which pairs exchange information about their experiences in real life. Similarly, Unit 1 step 4 contains a note-taking and listening activity on the theme of routines. This is followed by a presentation of the simple present tense as used in discussing routines. After writing answers to questions for controlled practice, students in pairs ask and answer their own questions on the theme of routines.

Language activities (stages 1 and 4)

The reading or listening steps which constitute the first stage are designed for authenticity and will frequently contain a considerable amount of new language. This is deliberate. In addition to introducing, in a communicative situation, the language to be presented and practised later, such passages help to develop in the students useful strategies for dealing with texts in which not all the language is known. The teacher may pre-teach some vocabulary, but should not lose sight of the aim of such steps: to extract and note down certain information only.

For the fourth stage, students will usually be sitting in pairs or groups. This arrangement gives maximum opportunity for free practice in a communicative situation. Students should not always work in the same pairs or groups. The size of the groups will depend on the size of the class and the task to be completed. The teacher should be prepared to vary the groups as the situation dictates; and to form a pair with an odd student when necessary. At the start of such activities, the teacher should always make sure that students understand what they are to do. And it is usually helpful to set a time limit. During the activity, the teacher may walk around the class to monitor progress, offering help where necessary but being tolerant of mistakes and trying not to interfere. Remember that in stages 1 and 4, *message* is more important than *language*. However, persistent and widespread errors should be noted for correction later. The teacher might then design additional remedial exercises and drills.

The role plays are designed to practise the language points covered in the earlier steps and to give students the opportunity to communicate meaningfully in English. To this end the authors adopt the information gap technique: certain information is given in the step itself, while other information is given at the end of the unit. Combined with the imagination of teacher and students, such a technique ensures lengthy and meaningful discussion. If necessary, students can be asked to prepare at home.

While it is not always necessary for roles to be assigned, a chairman or leader should normally be appointed for each group. The teacher should make sure that all students get the opportunity to be leader.

Drills (stage 3)

The laboratory drills are designed to provide controlled practice of language points. They are essentially mechanical but the authors have tried to give them a communicative value by setting them in a context and by varying the prompts. In some cases (see, for example, the first drill in Unit 1) intonation is being practised at the same time as a language point. The drills as recorded are three-phase: prompt, pause for student's response, correct response. The teacher may convert this into four-phase, with the students repeating the correct response, by pausing the tape after the correct response has been heard. Two or three examples are given at the beginning of each drill, with shorter pauses between prompt and correct response. The teacher may incorporate these examples into the drill itself by using the pause button to increase the pause for student response. Where necessary, students are referred to notes which will help them frame their responses. Drills are an example of controlled practice and the teacher should insist on accuracy (grammatical and intonational) at all times.

Specific notes for each step, answers to exercises and tapescripts of the recorded drills are provided in the unit-by-unit section of the Teacher's Book.

Syllabus

UNIT	FUNCTION	GRAMMAR STRUCTURE	TOPIC	ACTIVITY
1	asking and answering questions giving information routines and habits	simple present tense adverbs of frequency	company structure personal routines conferences	reading for information listening and note-taking group decision-making exercise
2	asking polite questions	indirect questions	conference agenda company performance letters of enquiry	pair work letter writing group activity
3	comparing and contrasting discussing advantages and disadvantages	simple comparisons intensifiers	air travel flight reservations offers and quotations	listening and note-taking role play group decision-making exercise
4	describing things and people measurements and calculations	prepositions	shapes, sizes, area, cost, calculations	listening and drawing gap-filling exercise pair work calculation exercise
5	sequencing criticizing	simple past tense *should/shouldn't have done*	factory layout newspaper reports insurance	role play listening and reading for information letter writing
6	describing trends dealing with statistics	simple past tense present perfect tense	graphs and statistics marketing budget	listening and drawing a curve discussing statistics interpreting figures writing a company profile

UNIT	FUNCTION	GRAMMAR STRUCTURE	TOPIC	ACTIVITY
7	giving instructions and directions obligation and necessity	modals (*must*/*mustn't*/ *needn't*/*don't have to* etc)	directions export regulations operating instructions credit cards job descriptions	pair work listening and note-taking writing a job description
8	describing processes	passive voice	car production house building memoranda	listening and note-taking group decision-making and problem-solving exercise memo writing
9	Consolidation exercises	Revision of Units 1 to 8		
10	future plans and intentions anticipating reactions	simple future tense *going to* and present continuous tense for future conditional 1 + *may*/ *might*/*could*	travel plans newspaper article energy saving	listening and note-taking true/false reading exercise group discussion and decision-making exercise memo writing
11	reporting and passing on information	reported speech— statements and questions	travel to the USA telephone messages overseas sales visit	listening and note-taking jigsaw reading exercise discussion
12	personal opinions agreeing and disagreeing putting a point and interrupting in meetings	*should*/*shouldn't*	meetings public opinion surveys	listening and note-taking pair work presenting ideas to a group discussion on company policy
13	complaining explaining and apologizing promises and offers	simple future tense for promises and offers *shall* with offers	delivery of goods problems with an order noise pollution	listening and note-taking role play gap-filling exercise
14	interviewing techniques asking for clarification placing emphasis	questions adjective order	job advertisements and interviews	listening and note-taking role play pair work

UNIT	FUNCTION	GRAMMAR STRUCTURE	TOPIC	ACTIVITY
15	advising and suggesting	gerund and infinitive *that* clauses conditionals + *may/ might*	investment shares, unit trusts and building societies	listening and note-taking information exchange reading for information decision-making exercise
16	comparing and contrasting evaluating alternatives expressing preferences	intensifiers superlatives adverbial expressions	renting accommodation quotations factory location	listening and note-taking telex writing decision-making exercise gap-filling exercise report writing
17	presentation techniques dealing with objections and queries referring to visual aids	inversion focussing passives	presenting a product visual aids order processing	listening and note-taking pair work presenting a point of view to a group and dealing with objections
18	Consolidation exercises	Revision of Units 9 to 17		
19	sequencing information evaluating information	revision of past tenses (simple past, present perfect, past perfect, past continuous) and passives	graphs and statistics entering a new market	gap-filling exercise listening and note-taking reading and note-taking vocabulary work group decision-making
20	requests and offers	modals simple futures indirect questions	phoning a travel agent negotiating an agreement with a foreign government medical care	controlled role play free role play letter writing listening and note-taking
21	certainty and uncertainty ability and achievement	*could/was able to* *must have/might have/ can't have*	sales visits company fortunes senior executive's illness	gap-filling exercise letter writing logical problem-solving case study

UNIT	FUNCTION	GRAMMAR STRUCTURE	TOPIC	ACTIVITY
22	plans and intentions rumours probability	simple future tense conditional 2 future continuous tense	setting up a new production plant Government plans making a film about the company economic trends	listening and note-taking discussing content of a film group work
23	chairing a meeting agreeing and disagreeing talking about suitability	*enough/too/such/so* + adjective	discussion of a new product machine specifications 'innovation for industry' competition	listening and note-taking role play report writing evaluation meeting
24	giving reasons making recommendations	connectors	office reorganization examining reasons for a company's decline	listening and note-taking controlled practice on connectors case study
25	permission prohibition restrictions regrets recriminations	modals past perfect tense conditional 3	advertising regulations advertising drugs and cigarettes losing a contract problems of an advertising agency	listening and note-taking reading for information group discussion letter writing
26	making arrangements sorting out problems	gerund and infinitive reported speech	problem in the technical sales department	problem-solving activity listening and note-taking gerund/infinitive exercise
27	Consolidation exercises	Revision of Units 20 to 26		

Unit-by-unit guide

1 The Executives' Conference (1)

1 Company details

Give students a minute or two to read the introductory paragraph. Make sure they understand the relationship between UMC, Ambermold International and Fittenwell Pharmaceuticals. Check that they all understand what they have to do.

Next ask them to look at the questionnaire. It is important that they understand all the terms used in the questionnaire, so pre-teach as necessary.

Arrange students into pairs to read the brochures and note down information. Explain that the language of the brochures is in authentic company brochure style and may be difficult in places. Students should not worry about unknown vocabulary, but skim-read to extract as quickly as possible information needed for the questionnaire. Set a realistic time-limit for reading.

At the end of the activity, each student should have filled out one of the columns in his questionnaire, as follows:

	Ambermold International	The Fittenwell Group
Date company established	25 years ago	15 years ago
Location of HQ	Manchester	Geneva, Switzerland
Date of take-over by UMC	end of last year	May last year
Number of employees	8,000	5,500
Main products	roller bearings	drugs and pharmaceutical preparations
Location of factories	Manchester, Greenock, Port Talbot	Zurich, Basel
Annual turnover	£22 million	250 million Swiss francs
Number of companies in group	five	three
Recent developments	—	manufacture of hospital and laboratory equipment
Future plans	development of new products opening new plant abroad modernizing existing factories	opening subsidiaries to assemble, market and distribute hospital equipment

2 Exchanging information

Present and practise the questions students will need to exchange information on the two companies. In particular, demonstrate that the formal language of the questionnaire is not appropriate to the discussion they are about to have. Instead of asking *At what date was the company established?* they should ask, less formally, *When was the company established?*

Allow a few minutes for each student to write down the questions he or she intends to ask. They should approximate to the following:

When was the company established?
Where are Ambermold's headquarters located?
When was the company taken over by UMC?
How many people work for Ambermold?/How many people are employed by Fittenwell?
What are the company's main products?
Where are their factories located?
What is the company's annual turnover?
How many companies are there in the group?
What recent developments have there been?/What new developments have there been recently?
What are the company's plans for the future?

Allow a few minutes for students, in pairs, to exchange their information on the company brochures, and to complete the second column in their questionnaires. They should then continue the information exchange by asking for and giving information about the companies they themselves work for and completing the third column in the questionnaire. Monitor the activity and check that students are using the question forms fluently and pronouncing new items correctly.

3 Vocabulary work

Ask students to do the exercise which refers to the brochure they read in step 1. Answers are as follows:

Ambermold International

Paragraph 1:
throughout
founded
comprises

Paragraph 2:
sealing
invention
sterile

Paragraph 3:
turnover

Paragraph 4:
funds
finally

Fittenwell Pharmaceuticals

Paragraph 1:
lengthy

Paragraph 2:
subsidiaries
laboratory

Paragraph 3:
recession
range

If the class has difficulty with the exercise, help them with clues; give the initial letters of the words they are to find, for example. To check understanding, ask individual students to make sentences containing these words. Point out that some of the words are rather technical and others formal and official.

4 Keith Andrews *(Tape section 1)*

The theme of step 4 is personal routines and job responsibilities and the grammar point is the simple present tense. Students are to listen to the tape in order to note down the information required. As in step 1, the text is designed for authenticity and it is spoken at normal speed. Pre-teach vocabulary only if you think students will not otherwise be able to extract the information needed.

Play the tape through without pauses and check on how much students have understood. Then play the tape again; this time students are to note down the information required. Pause the tape if necessary; in a particularly weak class, tell students what to listen for before restarting the tape (eg *Now he's going to give details of his working hours.*) Play the tape a third time if necessary, perhaps with a pause halfway through (after Job Responsibilities).

Ask individual students to report back from their notes. Here concentrate on the accuracy of their information rather than their language. If there is a general problem of understanding, quote the text and play that part of the tape again. The answers are:

Job title
  Quality control manager.

Job responsibilities
1 *To decide on sampling rate of finished goods.*
2 *To run tests on bearings sampled.*
3 *To set up tests and produce statistics.*

Working hours
  8.30–5.30 (¾ hour for lunch)

Working days
  Monday–Friday. On call one Saturday in three.

Meetings
  Monthly: report on quality control to boss.
  Weekly (Thursday afternoon): discuss technical matters with staff, also working conditions.

5 The simple present tense

Paradigms of the simple present tense and rules for its use are set out for students' reference. Draw their attention to the verb forms. Ask students to give other examples of the tense; if you wish, devise an additional exercise or drill for consolidation.

6 Questions

For controlled practice of the simple present, ask students to answer the questions about Keith Andrews.

The exercise can be written in class or at home, preceded by an oral stage. The answers are:

He works for Ambermold.
He never works on Sundays.
He attends monthly meetings and weekly meetings.
At the monthly meetings they discuss technical problems, trends in quality control, the defect rate, problems with customers, etc. At the weekly meetings they discuss technical matters and sometimes working conditions.
His first job responsibility is to decide on the sampling rate of finished goods.
He has ¾ hour for lunch (if he's lucky).

👥 Arrange students into pairs (or groups) for freer practice. Students are to ask and answer questions using the third person form. If you wish, start off by inviting questions from individual students and writing them up on the blackboard.

7 📼 At the Executives' Conference *(Tape section 2)*

The object of this step is for students to extract the questions the two executives ask. It is typical of the language used when two people meet socially on a formal occasion. Play the tape as many times as necessary; ask students to make a note of the questions and pause the tape periodically to allow them to do so. Refer them to the tapescripts in their books to check the answers:

And you're. . . ?
Where do you come from?
Whereabouts in Holland?
Where are you from?
Which part of UMC do you work for?
You make ball bearings, don't you?
And who do you work for?
So why are you here. . . ?

8 👥 Interviews

Arrange students into pairs to ask and answer similar questions. Since this is free stage practice, be tolerant of errors.

✏️ As optional follow-up, ask students to write a company journal style description of other students in the class. This can be set as a home assignment.

9 🎧 Drill 1: And Ambermold? *(Tape section 3/1)*

See page 6 of the introduction for instructions on the drills. Drill 1 offers controlled practice of simple present question forms and intonation. Insist on accuracy (both grammatical and intonational) and repeat the drill until this is achieved.

Tapescript:
You are trying to find out as much as possible about Ambermold.
You already have some information about Ambermold's competitors.
Use this as a basis for your questions.

I know there are seven companies in the Britsteel group.
How many companies are there in the Ambermold *group?*
I understand Sheffield Metals spend £12 million every year on new projects.
How much does Ambermold *spend every year on new projects?*

Notice that the word 'Ambermold' is emphasized. This is because facts about Ambermold are being contrasted with facts about other companies. Repeat again:

How many companies are there in the Ambermold *group?*
How much does Ambermold *spend every year on new projects?*

Now you go on in the same way:

As far as I know Sheffield Steel spends £5 million every year on research.
How much does Ambermold spend every year on research?
And I was told that Britsteel employs 400,000 people.
How many people does Ambermold employ?
I understand Sheffield Steel sells its products in the USA.
Where does Ambermold sell its products?
Apparently Britsteel HQ are located in Birmingham.
Where are Ambermold HQ located?
Of course Sheffield Steel's best known product is the SM24.
What is Ambermold's best known product?
I've heard that Industrial Metal import raw materials from the USSR.
Where does Ambermold import raw materials from?

🎧 Drill 2: Do you . . . ? *(Tape section 3/2)*

Drill 2 gives controlled practice in the use of adverbs and the simple present tense to talk about personal routines. When students have mastered the drill in the usual way, play the drill again, students this time giving true answers to the questions about spare-time interests.

Tapescript:
Somebody is asking about your spare-time interests. Listen:

Do you like going to the cinema?

Yes, I often go to the cinema.
Do you ever have a meal in a restaurant?
Yes, I occasionally have a meal in a restaurant.
Do you enjoy going to the opera?
No, I never go to the opera.

Each time use the notes to help you make sentences which show how regularly you go to the cinema, opera, and so on. Don't forget that the adverb of frequency (for example, *often, sometimes*) comes immediately after the subject—*I often go, I never visit.* . . .
Now you go on in the same way. The notes will help you.

Do you like going to the theatre?
Yes, I sometimes go to the theatre.
Do you enjoy visiting museums and art galleries?
No, I never visit museums and art galleries.
Do you ever go swimming?
Yes, I often go swimming.
Do you like walking in the country?
No, I hardly ever walk in the country.
Do you enjoy watching television in the evenings?
Yes, I nearly always watch television in the evenings.

10 The Marketing Conference

Arrange students into groups of four for the Marketing Conference role play; two students will read Provisional Programme A and two students will read Provisional Programme B (printed at the end of Unit 1 in the Student's book).

Make sure students understand what they are to do, and set a realistic time limit for them to read the programmes, discuss their merits and decide on compromises on timetabling, lecture, workgroups and film. Encourage students to talk from their own experience and to give their own opinions. Ask them to prepare for the role play at home if you wish.

The discussions should be monitored, but care must be taken in confronting students with their errors. At this stage of the unit, it is fluency which is being encouraged and too much correcting will be counter-productive in terms of motivation. It is best to pick one or two general mistakes (eg word order in indirect questions) and do remedial work on them afterwards.

11 Memo writing

This should not be lengthy. Discuss with students how to set out a memo. Emphasize that continuous prose is not essential. Elicit appropriate opening and closing sentences from the class and then set the exercise for homework.

2 The Executives' Conference (2)

1 📼 Arriving at the conference (Tape section 4)

Continuing the main theme of Unit 1, students are to listen to the conversation and note down the information given by the receptionist.
   Play the tape through without pauses and check on how much students have understood. Then play the tape again, this time students noting down the information given. Pause the tape if necessary and, in a particularly weak class, tell students what to listen for before restarting the tape. The receptionist gives the following information:

Conference hall opens at 8.30.
The first event isn't until 9.15.
It's a discussion about research budgeting.
The production managers' meeting is at 10.30 in Room B107.
The workshop session on marketing has been cancelled; there weren't enough people interested.
The telex number of UMC Sweden is S217364.

2 ✍ Could you tell me . . . ?

The same conversation can then be exploited for the polite way that Piet asks his questions. Ask students to listen out for these as you play the tape a third time; or, if you prefer, ask students to underline his questions in their tapescripts (near the end of Unit 2 in the Student's book).
   Now present the other polite question phrases and ask students to repeat them after you for fluency. Draw the students' attention to the transformations which must follow these phrases, and give them additional questions to transform in a similar way. Give additional practice in the *if* and *whether* question forms.

3 👥 Asking for information

Arrange students into pairs to practise the polite question forms presented in step 2. They should transform the questions as follows:

1 *Could you tell me where the Main Conference Hall is?*
2 *Can you tell me how much a single ticket to the airport is?*
3 *Do you know where I can buy a film for my camera?*
4 *Do you happen to know how long it takes by taxi?*
5 *I wonder if you could tell me who that is over there in the corner?*
6 *I'd like to know if you work for Ambermold or Fittenwell.*
7 *Would you mind telling me if telex facilities are available in this building?*

✏️ Ask students to write out their polite questions, at home or in class, for consolidation.

4 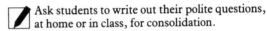 Conference agenda

Now that students have practised polite questions, arrange them into pairs to play the roles of conference delegate and receptionist. The delegate is to ask for the times and locations of the events on the work card. Set a time limit and ask pairs to change roles midway.

5 🎧 Drill 1: Is it true? (Tape section 5/1)

For controlled practice of a polite question form, students transform questions about the Ambermold Managing Director. See the introduction for instructions on the drills.

Tapescript:

A colleague has heard certain rumours about the Ambermold Managing Director. At the Executives' Conference you have a chance to find out if these rumours are true, when you meet a senior member of the Ambermold management team. For example, your colleague wants to know:

   Is the Managing Director hoping to go to Brussels soon?

So you ask the Ambermold Manager:

   Is it true that the Managing Director is hoping to go to Brussels soon?

   Has the Managing Director borrowed £15,000 from company funds?
   Is it true that the Managing Director has borrowed £15,000 from company funds?

Now you go on in the same way. Listen to the question from your colleague and then ask for confirmation from the Ambermold manager.

> Is the Managing Director planning a holiday from tomorrow?
> *Is it true that the Managing Director is planning a holiday from tomorrow?*
> Has he signed an agreement with Britsteel?
> *Is it true that he has signed an agreement with Britsteel?*
> Is he having talks with the Saudi Arabian government?
> *Is it true that he's having talks with the Saudi Arabian government?*
> Has he decided to appoint a woman as Chief Accountant?
> *Is it true that he's decided to appoint a woman as Chief Accountant?*
> Is he going to announce a large export contract?
> *Is it true that he's going to announce a large export contract?*
> Is he buying another Rolls Royce?
> *Is it true that he's buying another Rolls Royce?*

🎧 Drill 2: Yes, it is true! *(Tape section 5/2)*

Refer students to the notes in the Student's book ('your information'). The first two notes relate to the two examples given at the beginning of the drill. You may incorporate these into the drill if you wish, as explained in the introduction.

Tapescript:

You now have the information you want, so you can tell your colleague if the rumours about the Managing Director are true or not. Like this:

> So what did you find out while you were in Switzerland? Is it true about Brussels?
> *Yes, it is true that he's hoping to go to Brussels soon.*
> And the rumour about that large sum of money. Is that true?
> *No, it isn't true that he's borrowed £15,000 from company funds.*

Now you go on in the same way.

> And his holiday? Is that rumour true?
> *No, it isn't true that he's planning a holiday from tomorrow.*
> What they were saying about Britsteel, is that true?
> *Yes, it is true that he's signed an agreement with Britsteel.*
> What about Saudi Arabia? Was I right about that?
> *Yes, it is true that he's having talks with the Saudi Arabian government.*
> And the new Chief Accountant? Is that story true?
> *Yes, it is true that he's decided to appoint a woman as Chief Accountant.*

> And what about the export contract everybody's talking about? Is that right?
> *No, it isn't true that he's going to announce a large export contract.*
> But it is true about the new car, though, isn't it?
> *No, it isn't true that he's buying another Rolls Royce.*

6 ✏️ Letter writing

The aim of step 6 is to revise polite question phrases and to introduce the layout and style of business letters. Make sure students know that letters which begin *Dear Sir/Madam* always end in *Yours faithfully*; letters which start with the name of the addressee end in *Yours sincerely*. The letter writing part of the step requires students to substitute new references and requests for those in the model letter. Set as homework if you wish. Encourage students to use these and other polite forms:

We ... would be pleased to ...
Could you let us know ...
Could you tell us whether ...
We need to know ...

Their completed letters should approximate to the following:

Ambermold International
Swinton Lane
MANCHESTER M95 7TZ

__ May 19 __

Britsteel Limited
Britsteel House
Oakland Road
SHEFFIELD S3 4PJ

Dear Sir

We refer to your recent advertisement in the 'Iron and Steel Journal' for stainless steel casing units and would be pleased to receive your latest catalogue and price list. In particular, could you let us know the sizes and weights of the various units available. At the same time, could you tell us whether you consider that they are suitable for the manufacture of roller bearing systems.

Perhaps you could also let us know the circumstances under which you are prepared to grant discount facilities.

Thank you for your help.

Yours faithfully

7 🎭 UMC Directors in the hot seat

Introduce the role play by asking the class in general what questions they think should be put to the Directors. Prompt them if necessary with ideas about profits, turnover, company take-overs, factory closures and staff redundancy, diversification, new appointments, etc. Write these topics on the board for use in the role play.

👥 Divide students into groups of four, or into two larger groups if you prefer. One of the larger groups (or two students in each group of four) should take the roles of conference delegates and put questions, using polite question phrases, to the Directors. To make the role play more competitive, delegates have to try to get as much information as possible. Directors will only answer if they are questioned directly on a particular point. At the end, after about ten minutes, see how many facts UMC Directors have been able to keep secret.

3 More or less

1 📖 Flight details

Ask students to look at the flight information in their books. Ask a few questions to encourage skim-reading. Then ask students to compare airlines, using *quicker, slower, more frequent, earlier, more expensive*, etc. Ask individual students to use the structure *... not as (fast) as....*

Introduce the intensifiers *a lot, much, a great deal, a bit* and *a little* and ask individual students to make sentences with them.

2 Comparing

Present the comparatives and intensifiers and ask students to use them to make more sentences.

3 👥 Contrasting

Arrange students into pairs to continue controlled practice of comparatives and intensifiers. Start off by asking individual students to compare certain aspects of the five pairs of services. Look for answers like these:

1 *British Skyways flights are much more frequent than Overseas Airways.*
2 *Hawkwind Airlines are a great deal faster than Condor Airways.*
3 *Condor Airways are a little more expensive than Overseas Airways.*
4 *Inland Airways leave a lot earlier than Overseas Airways.*
5 *Hawkwind Airlines are much quicker than Inland Airways.*

Continue this oral practice with the *... not as ...* and *the only trouble is* structures.

✎ Now ask students, in pairs, to write sentences comparing the other five pairs of services in terms of the aspects dealt with above. Encourage them to help each other while writing; for example, one student could consult the flight information table while the other student writes down the sentences. They might then continue with a discussion of other pairs of services and other aspects.

4 👥 Which flight?

Arrange students into groups for this decision-making exercise. After the time limit, ask groups to report back on their decisions and how they were reached. They should also consider any disadvantages of the flights they choose, using the language presented in step 2.

5 📼 Seat reservations (*Tape section 6*)

In addition to listening out for the information required, students use the dialogue to revise polite requests and the phrases associated especially with telephoning (eg *Hold the line, I'll put you through to ...*).

Play the tape through without pauses and check on how much students have understood. Then play the tape again, this time students noting down the information required. Pause the tape if necessary. The information is:

Departure date: *Monday 19 March*
Time: *8.15 am*
Airline: *British Caledonian*
Flight: *BCL 241*
Ticket: *JB 248320*
Check-in time: *before 7.30 am*
Check-in place: *International departures desk*

6 👥 Calling the travel agent

Arrange students into pairs to recreate the dialogue they heard in step 5. If possible, record some of the students' dialogues and replay them to the class for comments.

7 Prepositions

For controlled practice in the use of prepositions, ask students to complete this exercise at home, or as a test in class. The completed text is as follows:

I'm flying to Frankfurt on British Airways flight number BA 743. It leaves Manchester at 10.30 on Friday 9 February and arrives in/at Frankfurt at 12.55 local time. I have to check in at the international departure terminal at least one hour before the aircraft is due to take off.

8 Drill 1: Frankfurt is better... *(Tape section 7/1)*

See page 6 of the introduction for instructions on the drills. Drill 1 offers controlled practice of comparatives and the intensifier *much*. Insist on accuracy and repeat the drill until this is achieved.

Tapescript

Listen to George Baxter and Christine Weber talking about their home cities.

> Manchester is a very expensive city, the most expensive in northern England.
> *Yes, but Frankfurt is much more expensive.*
> On the other hand, it's a nice place to live.
> *Yes, but Frankfurt is much nicer.*

Each time Christine Weber says that Frankfurt is very different from Manchester, she says it is *much nicer* or *much more expensive*. Now you go on in the same way. Imagine you are Christine Weber. Listen to what George Baxter has to say about Manchester and then say how Frankfurt is different.

> Manchester is a very important city, you know, as a business centre.
> *Yes, but Frankfurt's much more important.*
> And it's a very friendly place. Everybody says hello to you.
> *Yes, but Frankfurt's much more friendly.*
> And in Manchester there are lots of theatres, art galleries and cinemas. In fact, it's a very interesting city altogether.
> *Yes, but Frankfurt's much more interesting.*
> And the countryside near Manchester is quite beautiful.
> *Yes, but the countryside near Frankfurt is much more beautiful.*
> And the weather in Manchester is good you know. It hardly ever rains.
> *Yes, but the weather in Frankfurt is much better.*
> And don't forget football. Manchester's football team is very famous.
> *Yes, but Frankfurt's football team is much more famous.*
> Tell me something. What have you got against Manchester?

Drill 2: Yes, but... *(Tape section 7/2)*

Continuing the theme of comparisons of airlines, drill 2 practises a polite way of qualifying something that is said. Students respond with the help of the notes in their books.

Tapescript:

Your colleague is pointing out the advantages of travelling by different airlines. But you know that there are disadvantages. Tell your colleague about them. Like this:

> Skyways offer a very frequent service.
> *Yes, but on the other hand, their flights are rather expensive.*
> Hawkwind Airlines have the fastest flights.
> *Yes, but on the other hand, their flights are rather infrequent.*

Now you go on in the same way. The notes will help you:

> Inland Airways is amazingly cheap.
> *Yes, but on the other hand, their flights are rather long.*
> Skyways have no restrictions on return flights.
> *Yes, but on the other hand, their flights are rather early in the morning.*
> Overseas Airways offer an excellent cheap service if you can travel on Tuesday or Friday.
> *Yes, but on the other hand, their flights are rather late in the afternoon.*
> Hawkwind Airlines fly every day of the week.
> *Yes, but on the other hand, their flights are rather expensive.*
> Overseas Airways cost under £54.00. That can't be bad.
> *Yes, but on the other hand, their flights are rather infrequent.*
> Inland Airways offer a frequent and reliable service.
> *Yes, but on the other hand, their flights are rather long.*

9 Choosing a supplier

This role play involves a listening exercise and two texts which are to be read (one of these being at the end of the Unit in the Student's book).

First, arrange students into pairs to listen to tape section 8, and to complete the first column in their checklist. Play the tape as many times as necessary.

Now ask the pairs to read the letters and exchange information, so that all students have full information on all three suppliers and can complete their checklists accordingly. Here is the information required:

	Office Supplies	Candor Lighting	Brilight
Brand name	MAZODA	CANDOR SPECIAL FLUORTUBE	BRILIGHT
Price per item	£4.00 + VAT	£4.20 + VAT	£3.75 + VAT
Discount	10% on orders of over 50 tubes	5% on orders worth over £150 in any one month	—
Delivery period	2 weeks	2 weeks	28 days
Payment terms	against invoice within 30 days	net within 60 days	net 25 days after receipt
Guarantee	2,750 hours	3,500 hours	3,000 hours

Students now decide as a group which supplier should be given the order; they should use the language they have practised to compare and contrast and to talk about advantages and disadvantages. Set a time limit, monitor students' progress and follow up with remedial work on comparatives as necessary.

10 Letter writing

This can be done at home or in class. Remind students of the letter they wrote in Unit 2 step 6. Their letters should approximate to the following:

Purchasing Department
Ambermold International
Swinton Lane
MANCHESTER
M95 7TZ

Dear Sirs

Thank you for your offer recently received concerning fluorescent tubes. We would like to place a firm order for 55 MAZODA 150 watt tubes at a cost of £4.00 each, less 10% discount.

Please deliver the goods as soon as possible to the above address.

Yours faithfully

4 All shapes and sizes

1 🔲 Listen and draw (*Tape section 9*)

Students listen to descriptions on tape and draw simple diagrams. Ask individual students to describe their diagrams when they have finished. This will help you to find out how much of the language of dimension and relative position they already know. Their diagrams should be as follows:

a.

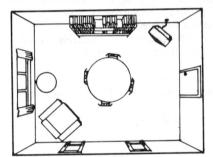

Total Area: 27 sq metres

b. A light switch

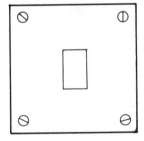

Total Area: 64 sq cm

c.

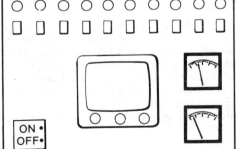

Total Area: 1750 sq cm

2 🔲 What's it like?

This step presents ways of describing objects and their relative positions. It can be extended to include radius and diameter, land area (hectares), imperial measurements (inches, feet, yards and miles) and weight (ounces, pounds, etc) depending on the level of the class. In addition, you can draw room plans, machines, etc, and ask individual students to describe them, to check fluency and vocabulary.

3 🔲 Prepositions

The completed paragraph is as follows:

> In *British* cars, the steering wheel is on *the right*. The horn is in *the middle* of *the wheel*. On *the extreme right* are the gauges: at *the top* is the temperature gauge, in *the middle* the oil gauge and at *the bottom* the fuel gauge. The ignition is next to *the fuel gauge*. Below *the steering wheel* are two switches and a button in *a row*. These are for *lights, windscreen wipers and for spraying the windscreen* with water to clean it. The bonnet release is not on *the dashboard itself, it is* under *it*.

For consolidation, ask individual students to describe their own cars.

The second part of the exercise can be done at home.

4 📖 What does he look like?

Give students a few minutes to study the description in their books; then ask questions to check understanding and fluency.

As an optional follow-up, show the class pictures of people; hold each one up for five seconds or so, then say that these people are all suspected of having committed a crime. Can they provide the police with a description? Afterwards, compare the descriptions with the pictures. Pre-teach simple past continuous (*he was carrying/he was wearing*) as a suitable tense for describing a person seen only fleetingly.

What is he like?

Give students a few minutes to read the description, as before. Then ask questions to check understanding and fluency. Next describe someone known to the entire class (eg politician, TV personality). Can they guess who it is from your description of his or her character? Name another well-known personality. Elicit from the class ways of describing his or her character. Make a list of suitable adjectives and phrases on the board.

Let students practise descriptions (of you and other students) in pairs, before writing their two paragraphs.

5 Describing

Students work in pairs to practise the language they have learnt for describing things and people.

6 Drill 1: How big . . . ? *(Tape section 10/1)*

The drill offers controlled practice in giving approximate measurements and weight. Students should refer to the drawings and give answers using *just under*, *just over* and *exactly*.

Tapescript:

Look at the drawings of two packages. You must give approximate information about their dimensions and weight. Like this:

> How wide is package A?
> *It's just under 30 cm wide.*
> And how long is it?
> *It's exactly 40 cm long.*
> And how much does it weigh?
> *It's just over 1,000 gms in weight.*

Now you go on in the same way.

> And how high is package A?
> *It's just over 20 cm high.*
> Now then, package B. How high is that?
> *It's just over 10 cm high.*
> And how much does it weigh?
> *It's just under 700 gms in weight.*
> And how long is it?
> *It's just over 80 cm long.*
> And finally, how wide is it?
> *It's exactly 20 cm wide.*

Drill 2: No . . . *(Tape section 10/2)*

Students are to respond with opposites of the cues: *left/right; bottom/top; horizontal/vertical*.

Tapescript:

You're talking to somebody who has all the wrong information about the design of the control panel for a new machine. Give her the correct information, like this. Listen:

> The light switches are on the left, aren't they?
> *No, they're on the right.*
> Oh yes. And the master switch is in the top right-hand corner, isn't it?
> *No, it's in the bottom left-hand corner.*

Now you go on in the same way.

> Oh yes, so it is. Now then, 50 cm is the vertical measurement, isn't it?
> *No, it's the horizontal measurement.*
> Oh dear. Erm, let's see. The clock is in the bottom left-hand corner, isn't it?
> *No, it's in the top right-hand corner.*
> Oh yes, of course. And the instructions are on the left, aren't they?
> *No, they're on the right.*
> Oh yes, so they are. Now then, let's have a look. 85 cm is the horizontal measurement, isn't it?
> *No, it's the vertical measurement.*
> Oh yes, that's right. And the video controls. I think I'm right in saying that they're at the top, aren't they?
> *No, they're at the bottom.*
> But the warning light is on the right-hand side, isn't it?
> *No, it's on the left-hand side.*
> Oh dear, now I'm completely confused.

7 Work it out!

Students work in pairs to exchange information and together find the answers. This exercise is intended to provide practice in manipulating figures and making calculations. For task (a), encourage students to use the letters to give measurements, eg AT is 15 cm, BC is 3 cm, etc. Make sure that each student looks at one diagram only. When all the information has been exchanged, there are still some gaps; but these can be worked out from the measurements already given. Throughout the step, to make sure that students talk about what they are doing, get them to discuss each stage of the calculations as they go. Alternatively, in a weak class, ask one student to write up the calculations on the board, with the whole class giving suggestions about how best to proceed. The quickest way to calculate the area is to take the total extreme area (15 cm × 8 cm = 120 sq cm) and subtract the sum of the areas of the missing rectangles (total area = 17 cm), giving a total surface area of 103 sq cm. Multiply this by the length of the piece (200 cm) and you have a total volume of 20,600 cubic centimetres, or 0.0206 cubic metres.

a) The dimensions are as follows:

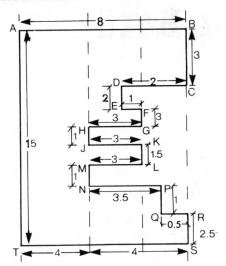

b) Total area = 103 sq cm
c) Total volume = 0.0206 cubic metres
d) Total cost = £0.5871

5 Disaster at Swinton Road

1 Factory layout *(Tape section 11)*

Following the usual procedure with note-taking exercises, play the tape through once and check on how much students have understood. Then play it again, with pauses if necessary. As an optional follow-up, ask students what the purpose of each department is and who works there. Ask students for similar descriptions of their factories or offices.

2 The phone rings... *(Tape section 12)*

A second listening exercise to develop the theme of the Unit. Check with students that they understand what has happened; play the tape again if necessary. Follow-up work is less important than maintaining the story line.

3 Press report

Point out in advance that newspaper English is difficult and different from ordinary spoken language. Tell students to note on their map the area damaged by the fire and Mrs Nutting's approximate position when she saw the fire. For follow-up, select similar stories from real newspapers and compare them. Also, vocabulary work: ask students to guess what *smouldering*, *wreaking havoc*, etc, mean.

4 The simple past tense and sequencing

Presentation of phrases used to sequence narrative. For consolidation, ask students how they made their breakfasts, came to school, etc.

5 Paragraph writing

Do this exercise orally first with the whole class, asking individual students for their suggestions. Then ask them to write the paragraph for homework. Completed paragraphs should look something like this:

The fire at Ambermold started late in the evening. Mrs Nutting left her house with her dog and walked along Swinton Lane. Suddenly she saw smoke and flames coming from the warehouse roof, so she telephoned the fire brigade. They left the fire station immediately. The next thing that happened was that Constable Jones telephoned Bill Owen of Ambermold to tell him about the fire. Bill Owen then telephoned Peter Jackson and told him the news. The fire brigade arrived at the factory, then Owen and Jackson arrived. In the end the fire brigade extinguished the fire. After that, the Evening Post reporters interviewed Inspector Cox. Finally the police, fire brigade and Ambermold managers left Swinton Road.

6 Questions to ask

This can be a simple mechanical exercise or can form the basis for a role play, students taking the parts of the reporter and the policeman. With a strong class, a good follow-up could be a free writing exercise in which students write a short newspaper-style report based on the policeman's answers.
  Here are the questions written out in full:

When did the fire break out?
What time did Mrs Nutting see the fire?
When did Mrs Nutting leave the house?
What is the Managing Director of Ambermold's name?
Which part of the factory did the fire destroy?
What time did the fire brigade arrive?
Why did the fire spread from the warehouse?
What time did the fire brigade extinguish the fire?
What is Mrs Nutting's address?

7 You didn't...

Presentation of *should/shouldn't have* form. Ask students to make up other similar sentences.

8 You should have...

Arrange students into pairs for controlled practice. Encourage them to use the contracted forms usual in speech:

1 *You should've locked the door.*
2 *You should've called the fire brigade.*

3 *You shouldn't have left paper on the warehouse floor.*
4 *You should've informed Mr Jackson about the fire.*
5 *You should've checked the fire extinguisher.*
6 *You should've closed the main door.*
7 *You shouldn't have left the key in the door.*
8 *You should've noticed the smoke coming from the roof.*

9 🎧 Drill 1: No, it didn't . . . (*Tape section 13/1*)

This offers controlled practice of negatives and intonation. Check the facts before starting so that students can give the correct information. Alternatively, write the cues on the blackboard. Excluding the examples, these are: *Swinton; Mrs; Ambermold; Cox; big.*

Tapescript:

You are the reporter from the *Manchester Evening Post*. Your boss, the Editor, has all the wrong information about the fire in Swinton Road. You must correct him. Listen:

> The fire started in the morning, didn't it?
> *No, it didn't. It started in the evening.*
> Mrs Nutting was out with her cat, wasn't she?
> *No, she wasn't. She was out with her dog.*

Stress the words 'evening' and 'dog' to show which part of your boss's information was incorrect. Now you go on in the same way:

> The fire was in Swanton, wasn't it?
> *No, it wasn't. It was in Swinton.*
> Mr Nutting telephoned the fire brigade, didn't he?
> *No, he didn't. Mrs Nutting telephoned the fire brigade.*
> Mr Jackson works for the fire brigade, doesn't he?
> *No, he doesn't. He works for Ambermold.*
> You interviewed Inspector Box, didn't you?
> *No, I didn't. I interviewed Inspector Cox.*
> Ambermold is a small factory, isn't it?
> *No, it isn't. It's a big factory.*

🎧 Drill 2: Yes, I realize . . . (*Tape section 13/2*)

This gives controlled practice in the use of *should/shouldn't have.*

Tapescript:

You are Peter Jackson, the Managing Director of Ambermold. You are talking to a representative of the insurance company after the disastrous fire at the Swinton Lane plant. Listen:

> You know, Mr Jackson, the fire door wasn't locked.
> *Yes, I realize the fire door should've been locked.*
> And private cars were parked outside. That's against the regulations, you know.
> *Yes, I realize private cars shouldn't have been parked outside.*

Now you go on in the same way:

> And another thing. The police weren't informed immediately.
> *Yes, I realize the police should've been informed immediately.*
> And the warehouse wasn't checked.
> *Yes, I realize the warehouse should've been checked.*
> And Gate 3 was locked, you know.
> *Yes, I realize Gate 3 shouldn't have been locked.*
> And the rubbish wasn't cleared away.
> *Yes, I realize the rubbish should've been cleared away.*
> And another thing. The hydrant wasn't repaired.
> *Yes, I realize the hydrant should've been repaired.*
> And apart from anything else, we weren't contacted immediately.
> *Yes, I realize you should've been contacted immediately.*

10 🎭 Meeting the insurers

This needs a substantial amount of preparation. Ambermold have two documents: their detailed claim and extracts from letters and record cards which support their view that the claim should be settled in full. The Insurance Company has an annotated map showing Ambermold's mistakes. There is no need to allocate specific roles, but it is necessary to nominate leaders of each team.

At the beginning of the meeting, Ambermold present their claim by showing their report on the damage. The Insurance Company present and comment on their annotated map.

The aim of the role play is to reach agreement on a compromise settlement. Ambermold use their documents to support their argument that the sprinkler system was in order, and that it was agreed with the police that Gate 3 should be locked. Other excuses have to be invented for the other mistakes.

11 ✍ Letter writing

Following compromise agreement, students insert into the letter reasons for refusal to settle in full and also propose a final settlement amount.

Optional follow-up: Ambermold write to accept or reject this proposed settlement. Ask students to write this letter at home.

6 Facts and figures

1 🎧 The sales graph (Tape section 14)

Students listen to the tape and plot the curve. With a weaker class, pre-teach the use of *from*, *by* and *to* with figures in order to avoid confusion. The sales graphs should be as follows:

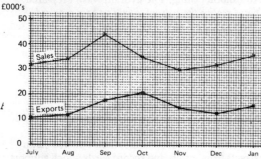

2 Describing trends

Other verbs can be introduced: *rocket* and *plummet*, *shoot up* and *slump* and also *level off*, *peak*, *high* and *low point*. Weaker classes can write simple sentences such as:

Sales went up from £32,000 to £34,000 in August.
Sales went up by £2,000 in August.

3 The chairman's report

Students should underline these adverbs:

slightly, substantially, sharply, slightly, slowly, steadily

If you wish, continue with an adverb/adjective transformation exercise. For example:

Sales rose slightly.
There was a slight rise in sales.

4 Describing trends with adverbs

Stress that there is no absolute relation between the angle of the curve and the use of a particular adverb. Discussion point: show how the same set of statistics can be presented differently by, for example, extending the vertical or horizontal axes to suggest sharp or gradual increases.

5 Describing graphs

Ask students to write their paragraphs at home or set them as a test in class. Their paragraphs should be like the following:

1 *At the beginning of the period, sales were low at 11,000. They rose in August to 12,000 and in September to 18,000, an increase in one month of 6,000. In October they rose by only 3,000 to reach a high point of 21,000. In November they fell back to 15,000 and in December they were lower again at 13,000. In January they went up again by 3,000 to reach 16,000 at the end of the period.*

2 *Exports were low at the beginning of the period. They rose slightly in August and then went up dramatically in September. They then levelled off although there was a small increase in October. In November and December they fell gradually and recovered slightly in January, ending the period substantially higher than in July.*

6 Drawing graphs

Revise useful adverbs before the activity. If necessary, write them up on the blackboard to help weaker students.

7 Drill 1: Up and down.. (Tape section 15/1)

This offers controlled practice in the use of six verbs commonly used to describe financial trends. In each case, students are to respond with the verb which is the opposite of the verb in the cue. All the responses should begin with the polite phrase *As a matter of fact...* and the change is always *by 50%*.

Tapescript:

When we are talking about the changes in the fortune of a company we use some of the following verbs:

go up and its opposite *go down*
increase and its opposite *decrease*
rise and its opposite *fall*

Now listen. Somebody is being corrected. She thinks that certain things happened to the company but the person talking to her knows that the opposite is true.

> Sales went up last year, didn't they?
> *As a matter of fact they didn't. They went down by 50%.*
> Total production fell last year, didn't it?
> *As a matter of fact it didn't. It rose by 50%.*

Now you go on in the same way.

> New orders went down last year, didn't they?
> *As a matter of fact they didn't. They went up by 50%.*
> Government subsidies decreased last year, didn't they?
> *As a matter of fact they didn't. They increased by 50%.*
> Prices fell last year, didn't they?
> *As a matter of fact they didn't. They rose by 50%.*
> And taxes went down last year, didn't they?
> *As a matter of fact they didn't. They went up by 50%.*
> And shares. They rose, didn't they?
> *As a matter of fact they didn't. They fell by 50%.*

Drill 2: Yes, that's right... (*Tape section 15/2*)

More practice with the same verbs. In this case, students are to respond with the verb they hear in the cue, and to say by how much things have changed.

Tapescript:

You are talking to a colleague about recent changes affecting the company. You confirm that he has the right information this time. Like this. Listen.

> Prices of the ZB12 went up from £25 to £30 last year, didn't they?
> *Yes, that's right. They went up by £5.*
> But monthly sales fell from £12,000 to £10,000.
> *Yes, that's right. They fell by £2,000.*

Each time you have to say *by how much* things have changed. Now go on in the same way.

> Share prices went up from 200 pence to 250 pence, didn't they?
> *Yes, that's right. They went up by 50 pence.*
> New orders went up from 150 to 175 last year, didn't they?
> *Yes, that's right. They went up by 25.*
> Sales to the USA increased from £50,000 to £60,000, didn't they?
> *Yes, that's right. They increased by £10,000.*
> And subsidies decreased from £16,000 to £10,000, didn't they?
> *Yes, that's right. They decreased by £6,000.*
> Exports to the EEC went down from £80,000 to £50,000, didn't they?
> *Yes, that's right. They went down by £30,000.*

8 The present perfect tense

Make sure students understand the difference between the two tenses and invite them to make up more sentences. In addition it might be helpful to compile with students two lists of time expressions—one for finished time, one for unfinished time—to help them decide whether simple past or present perfect is appropriate, eg:

finished: *in 1964, last Christmas, three days ago, yesterday;*
unfinished: *this year, so far, this month, until now.*

9 Last year and this year

Do this exercise orally first: ask students to make up sentences, using the present perfect tense, from the information given in the brackets.

Then ask students to write down their sentences, either at home or in class. They are as follows:

1 *This year prices have risen by 12%.*
2 *This year sales have increased by 8%.*
3 *This year exports to the USA have fallen by 5%.*
4 *This year home sales have improved by 9%.*
5 *This year profits have dropped by 4%.*
6 *This year inflation has gone up by 1%.*
7 *This year exports to the EEC have gone up by 9%.*
8 *This year taxes have risen by 12%.*

10 Finding a market

Students work individually during the information transfer stage. A curve for Brazil has to be added to each of the four graphs, based on information in the passage.

Remedial work: ask students to describe the curves for, say, Germany, to practise use of simple past/present perfect. Vertical line in the middle of each graph divides 'last year' from 'this year'.

11 Allocating the marketing budget

Allow some time for preparation. Students have to use information on graphs plus their own knowledge of economic factors to surmise which will be the most lucrative market for their products.

12 History of the company

A weaker class can be asked simply to form individual sentences from the information given, rather than put together a connected paragraph.

7 Here's how

1 🎧 Giving directions (*Tape section 16*)

If necessary, pre-teach the language of giving directions (see tapescript in the Student's Book), using the 1st Floor Plan.

2 ✋ Asking for and giving directions

This is a good opportunity to revise the polite question forms covered in Unit 2. Ask students to ask and answer more questions, exploiting the Floor Plan in their books.

3 ✋ Vocabulary work

Set this exercise as a test on the following day. The complete text is as follows:

Can you tell me the way to Mrs Bowden's office, please?
Yes, I think so. You go straight along here to the end. Then you turn left and immediately right. Go through the double doors and it's the second door on the left.

Do you know where Mr Payne's office is, please?
Yes, go up the stairs to the first floor. Go along the corridor, the first right and it's the first on your left.

4 👥 Can you tell me the way?

Students continue to practise directions, as in step 2, this time in pairs.

5 🎧 Exporting to Europe (*Tape section 17*)

Note-taking and listening exercise. The answers are:

	EEC	Eastern Europe
Shipping documents	Yes	Yes
Insurance policy	Yes	Yes
Import licence	No	Yes
Metric measurements	Yes	No
Translations	No	Yes
Notification to customs	Yes	Yes
Notification to Board of Trade	No	Yes

Students can look at the tapescript after the exercise has been completed, and underline different ways of saying that something is, or is not, necessary.

6 ✋ Rules and regulations

For students' reference. If you wish, ask students to make up more sentences based on the tape.

7 ✏️ Necessary or not?

Ask students to write sentences at home. If necessary, give them some ideas in class beforehand.

8 👥 Exchanging information

Britnat Credit Card

Students asking for information could spend some time in groups discussing the points they want to raise. A weaker class may need some prompting from the teacher in the form of a checklist of questions.

Drilling Machine

The 'trainers' may need some help with the vocabulary. It may be useful to show students a picture of a drilling machine and discuss its various parts and the operations it can perform, before embarking on the pair work exercise.

Here are the words and phrases for the vocabulary section:

1. non-transferable
2. annual
3. interest
4. applicant
5. mains supply
6. debris
7. chuck key
8. switch
9. jam

9 🎧 Drill 1: Is it necessary? (*Tape section 18/1*)

For practice in talking about regulations. In each case, students respond with: *Oh no, you don't have to....*

Tapescript:

Listen to these people talking about regulations as they apply to a foreign country.

> Is it necessary to apply for a visa if I want to stay in your country?
> *Oh no, you don't have to apply for a visa.*
> And is it necessary to have a health certificate?
> *Oh no, you don't have to have a health certificate.*

Now you go on in the same way:

> And what about an identity card. Is it necessary to have one?
> *Oh no, you don't have to have an identity card.*
> And do you think it's necessary to take out an insurance policy?
> *Oh no, you don't have to take out an insurance policy.*
> What about the tax position? As a foreigner, is it necessary to pay VAT on luxury goods?
> *Oh no, you don't have to pay VAT on luxury goods.*
> And what about driving? Is it necessary to apply for an international driving licence?
> *Oh no, you don't have to apply for an international driving licence.*
> And is it true that I must leave the country within a certain time?
> *Oh no, you don't have to leave the country within a certain time.*
> Just one more question. Is it necessary to book flights to your country one month in advance?
> *Oh no, you don't have to book flights one month in advance.*
> Thank you very much. You've been most helpful.

◯ Drill 2: How to do it *(Tape section 18/2)*

For further practice in talking about regulations. Students use notes to respond with: *Yes, you must. . . .* or *No, you mustn't. . . .*

Tapescript:

You're answering somebody's questions about a machine which was recently installed at your factory. Look at the list of **do's** and **don'ts** in your book and listen to these examples:

> I've got some questions about this machine. Does it matter if I don't follow all the operating instructions?
> *Yes, you must follow all the operating instructions.*
> And can I allow untrained operators to use the machine?
> *No, you mustn't allow untrained operators to use the machine.*

Now you go on in the same way:

> What about repairs? Can we try to repair the machine if it breaks down?
> *No, you mustn't try to repair the machine if it breaks down.*
> And do we have to keep the machine clean at all times?
> *Yes, you must keep the machine clean at all times.*
> And someone said we had to check the plug before switching on? Is that really necessary?
> *Yes, you must check the plug before switching on.*
> By the way, is it all right to open the top while the machine is operating?
> *No, you mustn't open the top while the machine is operating.*
> And we've got a small room where we want to use the machine. Is that OK?
> *No, you mustn't use the machine in a small room.*
> What about overhauling? Is it strictly necessary to overhaul the machine every six months?
> *Yes, you must overhaul the machine every six months.*
> Is it absolutely necessary to switch off at the mains every night?
> *Yes, you must switch off at the mains every night.*
> The last thing I want to know is this. Is it all right for us to leave the machine unattended while switched on?
> *No, you mustn't leave the machine unattended while switched on.*

10 👥 Job descriptions

Start if necessary by asking students to read the Overseas Sales Manager's job description (step 11) and to make notes on his duties. Discuss as a class. Then divide into groups; each group produces a similar checklist for two of the other posts. Follow this by class discussion on accuracy of the lists compiled. The language of *doesn't have to, has to,* etc, should arise naturally.

11 📖 The OSM

(See notes for step 10 above.)

✏️ Writing a job description

Don't expect students to be able to write a job description exactly like the one given. Ask for a maximum of ten sentences suitable for inclusion in a letter to an applicant for the post in question.

12 👥 Twenty questions

Don't monitor grammatical accuracy too closely. In activities of this kind students should sometimes have the opportunity to talk without feeling that they must strive for 100% accuracy.

8 No sooner said than done!

1 🎧 Car production (Tape section 19)

Listening and note-taking exercise. Focus on successful completion of task. Students can be asked to report back on the information they have noted down. This will give an indication of how familiar they are with the passive voice.

Details given on tape are as follows:

	France	England
Total number of cars produced last year	1,750,000	1,225,000
Total number of cars to be produced this year (estimate)	2,000,000	1,100,000
Location of factories	Paris, Lyon	Birmingham, Oxford, London
Parts imported	glass—Czechoslovakia, tyres—West Germany	seats—Ireland
Percentage of cars exported last year	35%	23.5%
Percentage of cars to be exported this year (estimate)	34%	17%

2 👍 The passive

Rules of use. Elicit further examples of passive sentences based on the tape.

3 👥 Production statistics

Make sure students know the time perspective. X marks present time. The dotted lines on the *Sales of Wine* diagram for years 5, 6, and 7 indicate future time.

4 👍 Processes

This can be done orally in class. Look for sentences like these:

After the house has been designed, planning permission is granted.
After planning permission has been granted, a builder is asked to give an estimate.
After the estimate has been accepted, a contract is signed.
After the contract has been signed, the house is built.
After the house has been built, it is offered for sale.

5 ✏️ Buying and selling goods

Set for homework. A weaker class will write unconnected sentences. More advanced classes can be expected to write a full paragraph, in which case emphasize that it is not necessary to copy the format in step 4 exactly (see below).

The correct order of the stages is:

enquiry, offer, order, confirmation, acknowledgement, documents, packing, dispatch, delivery, invoice, payment.

After an enquiry has been received, an offer is prepared and sent to the enquirer. If the offer is acceptable, an order is placed. If the order is placed by telephone it must be confirmed in writing. The order is acknowledged by the supplier, documents are prepared and, when the goods are ready, they are packed, dispatched and delivered to the buyer's address. An invoice is prepared and sent to the buyer. The invoice is paid a certain number of days after receipt.

6 🎧 Car manufacture (Tape section 20)

Listening for specific information. The higher the level of the class, the greater the amount of detail the students can be expected to note down. The six departments are:

cutting, pressing, welding,
assembly, spraying, quality control.

7 Drill 1: And what about . . . ? (Tape section 21/1)

Students use the notes in their books to respond with the simple present passive.

Tapescript:

Listen to Alan Davies answering questions about car production at British Autocar's Birmingham plant.

> Is the spraying done by the workers?
> *No, the cars are sprayed by robots.*
> And what about testing? Is that done in the main factory?
> *No, the cars are tested in the quality control department.*

Now you go on in the same way. The notes will help you.

> And what about design? Is all that done in America?
> *No, the cars are designed here in Birmingham.*
> I see. Tell me about assembly. Is that done automatically?
> *No, the cars are assembled manually.*
> And is the welding done in this department?
> *No, the cars are welded in that department over there.*
> What about distribution? That's normally done by rail I suppose?
> *No, the cars are distributed by road transporter.*
> And sales? I imagine you have your own sales network.
> *No, the cars are sold in private showrooms.*
> I should think only rich people could afford to buy your cars.
> *No, the cars are bought by all sorts of people.*

Drill 2: Yes, but . . . (Tape section 21/2)

Students use the notes to respond with the present perfect passive.

Tapescript:

Listen to these two people talking about a new product. Each time the second person points out that an earlier stage of production is important.

> I think we should market the product immediately.
> *Yes, but not until it's been properly developed.*
> I think we should launch the product as soon as possible.
> *Yes, but not until it's been thoroughly tested.*

Now you go on in the same way. The notes will help you.

> I'm convinced we should start exporting the product to EEC countries.
> *Yes, but not until it's been tried out here in the UK.*
> I think we should advertise the product in the national press.
> *Yes, but not until it's been presented at the Trade Fair.*
> And we could offer a range of accessories to the product.
> *Yes, but not until it's been accepted by the market in its present form.*
> And I think we should invite journalists to have a look at it.
> *Yes, but not until it's been shown to important potential customers.*
> And we should sell it nationwide.
> *Yes, but not until it's been sold in the south east.*
> And one more thing. I'm in favour of printing the catalogue in eight languages.
> *Yes, but not until it's been printed in English.*

8 Action taken

Make sure students understand the use of the reduced form of the passive for notes. Ask them to reduce other passive sentences as you give them.

For the second section, set a strict time limit (about three minutes) on the discussion of each point. Make sure that students note down their decision fully, so that they have enough material for step 9.

9 Memo writing

Students base their memos on the example given, using notes from step 8.

9 Consolidation exercises

These can be set as a formal test to check learning of language in the first eight units. Exercises 1, 7 and 8 allow only one correct answer. The other exercises allow the student some freedom. The key gives models of suitable answers.

Alternatively they can be used as extra remedial exercises to reinforce the structures being taught in each unit; for example, exercise 2 could be given to a class having difficulty with the use of intensifiers in Unit 3. Exercise 6 could be set as homework during the teaching of Unit 7.

Some of the exercises could be developed into role play or decision-making exercises if required, for example, exercises 2, 3 and 7.

KEY

1 ✎ The foam experts

1 was founded
2 has expanded
3 announced
4 are sold
5 is represented
6 went
7 was taken over
8 is cooled
9 is injected
10 offer
11 guarantee
12 have improved
13 contact
14 look

2 ✎ Figures

Petroplas' turnover was much higher last year than Baxcel's.
Petroplas' profit before tax was a lot higher last year than Baxcel's.
Baxcel can supply slightly more grades of foam than Petroplas.
Petroplas' production was a great deal higher last year than Baxcel's.
Petroplas has been in business a lot longer than Baxcel.
Petroplas employs slightly more people than Baxcel.
Baxcel's products are a bit cheaper than Petroplas'.

3 ✎ Telephone messages

Can you tell me if you produce foam suitable for car seats?
Could you tell me what the foam is made of?
Do you know how far it is to your nearest factory or warehouse?
I'd like to know what discount facilities are available.
Can you tell me what your average delivery period is?
I wonder if you could tell me what guarantees there are on your products.
I need to know if the foam is resistant to fire.
Can you tell me how much the foam costs per cubic metre?

4 ✎ Details

The single seat foam block measures 70 cm × 45 cm × 5 cm and is priced at £4.50 and the double is 105 cm × 70 cm × 5 cm and costs £8.25. We are able to offer a discount of 10% on these prices if the total value of your order is over £100.00.

We assure you of our best attention and prompt delivery of all goods ordered.

5 ✎ Statistics

Over the last five years the safety of our products has improved substantially. This can be seen from the dramatic fall in the number of fires involving Baxcel products. For the first two years the number of fires was constant at about 200 per year but following the addition of anti-fire chemicals to the foam at the beginning of the third year the number fell to about 150 and the situation improved further at the beginning of this year when more effective chemicals were added. The present level of fires is about 100 per year and we hope that this positive trend will continue in the future.

6 ✎ Getting there

If you are coming on the M62 motorway from Manchester you turn off at Junction 17 and follow the signs for Garforth. You go over a roundabout and then take the third turning on the left. Then take the first right and the main entrance to Baxcel is on your left just after a side road.

7 ✏ Problems

You should have stored the foam according to instructions.
You should have cut the foam correctly.
You shouldn't have used cheap glue to stick the foam to the seat.
You should have informed us immediately of the problem.
You should have asked our advice about how best to assemble the seats.
You shouldn't have covered the seats with cheap synthetic material.
You should have checked the seats before they left the factory.

8 ✏ We regret...

On 19 January we started using your foam *in* our car seats. *At* that time we were producing *at* least 220 seats *per* day. We were very satisfied *with* the foam *at* first but soon we started receiving complaints *from* our main customers, British Autocars Ltd.

In view *of* the fact that you do not accept responsibility *for* the defects, we have decided not *to* purchase any further stocks *from* your company.

We will return your latest consignment *as* soon *as* possible. Please cancel our order *of* 14 September *for* 1000 pieces of foam (size AB20).

10 Plans, arrangements and decisions

1 ▣ Next week's programme (*Tape section 22*)

Listening and note-taking exercise. The details of David Barker's programme are as follows:

Monday: Hans Weber—Manchester
Tuesday: *Fly to Milan 8.30. Visit Milan Factory. Train to Turin 6.00. Hotel Splendide, Turin.*
Wednesday: *Conference in Turin. Fly to Vienna 4.30 (if no call from England).*
Thursday: *Lunch—Herr Richard. Either factory visit or discuss agency contract.*
Friday: *Museums/art galleries; evening—opera/theatre.*
Saturday: *Fly to Manchester. British Airways 9.00.*

2 ☝ The present continuous tense and
3 ☝ The simple future tense

For students' reference. Ask students to give other, similar sentences to check understanding.

4 ✎ Discussing plans

Students expand their notes from step 1 and write complete sentences using the present continuous and simple future tenses as presented in step 2 and step 3.

5 ☻ What about you?

After discussing Bob Grant's and Nancy Harding's plans, students can ask each other about their own plans for the future and report back to the class.

Throughout steps 2, 3, 4 and 5, draw a sharp distinction between finalized plans and vague hopes and possibilities. Insist that the present continuous is used for the former and the simple future + *perhaps* or *I hope* for the latter.

Going to is not taught here. If the class can cope with another exponent, point out that *going to* is used to communicate intention or inevitability.

I'm going to talk today about our marketing policy.
We're going to make a loss this year.

6 ▯ The new helicopter

Reading for information; to present *could*, *may* and *might* contrasted with *will*.

7 ▯ True or false?

To highlight the language of talking about future plans and intentions. The answers are:

1 *True.*
2 *False.* *It will carry* up to *40 passengers.*
3 *True.*
4 *False.* *It will cost £750 million.*
5 *False.* *It is possible; 2000 jobs may be created.*
6 *True.*
7 *False.* *It is not certain. The aircraft could be powered by engines made in Britain, France or the United States.*

8 ☝ Possibilities and probabilities

Presentation, for students' reference, of simple future tense (active and passive) for facts and decisions and the modals *may*, *might* and *could* (with passive) to discuss future probabilities and possibilities.

9 ✎ The simple future passive

Students write sentences using *will*, *could*, *may* and *might*, like the following:

1 *A new plant may be set up in South America.*
2 *Annual wage rises will be discussed before the end of next month.*
3 *A new version of the ABS bearing system will be produced within five years.*
4 *The production area at the Swinton Lane plant could be extended.*
5 *A new contract will be negotiated with the Indonesian government.*
6 *American motors might be used to operate the new production line.*

7 *The potential of the Scandinavian market* will *be investigated.*
8 *50 office workers* may *be made redundant at Swinton Lane.*

10 🎧 Drill 1: Tell me (*Tape section 23/1*)

To practise the present continuous tense for future plans. Students use the notes in their books.

Tapescript:

Look at Peter Milne's diary for the coming week. Now listen to these examples.

> When exactly are you leaving for Geneva, Peter?
> *Oh, I'm leaving for Geneva at 2.30 on Monday.*
> I see. And when exactly are you meeting Herr Richard?
> *Oh, I'm meeting Herr Richard at 5.00 on Monday.*

Now imagine that you are Peter Milne. Answer your secretary's questions about your business trip.

> And when exactly are you meeting the Managing Director of Metalco?
> *Oh, I'm meeting the Managing Director of Metalco at 10.00 on Tuesday.*
> What about the Trade Fair? When are you attending that?
> *Oh, I'm attending the Trade Fair in Montreux at 2.00 on Tuesday.*
> Oh yes, now you mentioned a game of golf with David. When's that?
> *Oh, I'm playing golf with David at 12.00 on Wednesday.*
> And of course you'll be having dinner with him, won't you? What time's that planned for?
> *Oh, I'm having dinner with David at 7.30 on Wednesday.*
> And on Thursday it's back to London. What time exactly?
> *Oh, I'm leaving for London at 9.15 on Thursday.*
> So when do you report back to the managers?
> *Oh, I'm reporting back to the Ambermold managers at 3.00 on Thursday.*
> Well, I hope you have an enjoyable time. See you on Thursday.

🎧 Drill 2: And this year? (*Tape section 23/2*)

For practice in the simple future tense.

Tapescript:

Listen to these two people talking about events in the company calendar.

> Last year the company announced profits on 19 June, I think.
> *When will they be announced this year?*
> Oh, around the same date I suppose. And the annual conference, they held that in Blackpool last year.
> *Where will it be held this year?*

Each time the second person asks a question using the passive form of the verb. Now you go on in the same way:

> Of course they published the accounts at the end of July last year.
> *When will they be published this year?*
> At the end of June. And then they held talks with the unions in August.
> *When will they be held this year?*
> During August sometime, I imagine. And they announced the half-year figures in London last year.
> *Where will they be announced this year?*
> In Berlin at the Trade Fair, as far as I know. Last year they released details of export contracts in January.
> *When will they be released this year?*
> Probably towards the end of January. Of course they won't want to delay the sales campaign this year.
> *When will it be launched this year?*
> Early February is my guess. Still, there's always the office party to look forward to. Do you know, they sent out the invitations in September last year.
> *When will they be sent out this year?*
> Well, quite honestly I wouldn't be surprised if they sent them out in the middle of June!

11 📖 Save it!

Read the report as a class. Make sure all students understand the options open.

👥👥 Then divide into groups for the decision-making exercise. Discuss the various decisions with the whole class. Ask the class to anticipate the reaction of the workforce, and the effect of their decisions. This should bring in the use of the first conditional.

12 ✏️ Writing a memo

Each group could work on writing one memo. This should make the task easier.

11 Go West, young man!

1 🔲 Immigration procedures in the USA
(*Tape section 24*)

Listening and note-taking exercise followed by mechanical transformation exercises (direct question → reported question).

1 Length of stay in US.
2 Business or tourist?
3 Address in US.
4 Address in UK.
5 Money held in travellers' cheques and cash.
6 Ever been to a psychiatrist?

✏️ For the second part of step 1, students should write the following questions:

1 *How long are you staying in the United States?*
2 *Are you here on business or as a tourist?*
3 *Have you an address in the United States?*
4 *Where do you live in the UK?*
5 *How much money do you have in travellers' cheques and cash?*
6 *Have you ever been to a psychiatrist?*

To see if students can make direct question/reported question transformations, ask them what the immigration officer wanted to know. Expect answers like these:

The immigration officer wanted to know:
1 *how long I was staying in the US.*
2 *whether I was there on business or as a tourist.*
3 *whether I had an address in the US.*
4 *where I lived in the UK.*
5 *how much money I had in travellers' cheques and cash.*
6 *if I had ever been to a psychiatrist.*

This last part is a diagnostic exercise to ascertain whether this particular grammar point needs to be taught.

2 📖 Reporting questions

Transformation rules for students' reference. If you wish, make up some questions for the students to transform orally.

3 ✏️ Press report

For practice in direct/indirect question transformations.
Ask students to write out their indirect questions at home. They are as follows:

1 *He asked me what my full name was.*
2 *He asked me how old I was.*
3 *He asked me where I lived.*
4 *He asked me if I could describe the events of the morning of 23 July.*
5 *He wanted to know what I thought when the robber pointed a gun straight at me.*
6 *He wanted to know how I got the gun off him.*
7 *He asked me what happened when the police arrived.*
8 *He wanted to know if I received any reward from the bank.*
9 *He asked me what my wife and family thought about the whole episode.*
10 *He wanted to know if I was afraid of going into a bank now.*

👥 Alternatively, get students to practise the transformations in pairs.

4 📖 Arrangements for a trip

You may first need to revise the questions the US immigration officer asked (see step 1).

5 🔲 The immigration officer (*Tape section 25*)

Best done in the language laboratory, using the memo as a cuesheet.

6 👥 Reporting back

This can become a mini role play, based on tape section 25. Play the tape again at the beginning of the activity, if you wish. One student should ask questions, the other give replies like these:

He asked me how long I was planning to stay in the USA.
He wanted to know if I had an address there.
He asked me if I was there on business or as a tourist.
He wanted to know how much money I had with me.
He asked me who I worked for.
He wanted to know if I had ever been a member of the Communist Party.

7 👥 Who's getting the contract?

The interview with Burley H. Crawford could be reconstructed. Situation: News conference. The world's press ask BHC questions and note down his responses. The teacher can play BHC if the class is of lower level. Students then report BHC's statements, perhaps writing a short article as follow-up.

8 Reporting statements

Presentation of verbs commonly used for reporting statements. Give students statements to transform orally.

9 Telephone messages

Controlled practice in reported speech. Students could go on to invent their own telephone calls, note down messages and report them.

10 Drill 1: What did they ask? (*Tape section 26/1*)

For controlled practice in transforming direct questions into indirect questions. Students use the notes in their books.

Tapescript:

You have just been interviewed for a job. In your book is part of the form you had to fill in. Tell a friend about the questions you had to answer:

> So what did they ask you?
> Well, *they wanted to know if I had worked in a similar job before.*
> I see. And what about qualifications?
> Well, *they wanted to know what relevant qualifications I had.*

Now you go on in the same way:

> Oh yes, what else?
> Well, *they wanted to know why I was looking for a new job.*
> Oh did they? What did they ask you about your present job?
> Well, *they wanted to know what I liked most about my present job.*
> Oh yes, anything else?
> Well, *they wanted to know what I liked least about my present job.*
> I see. What else did they want to know?
> Well, *they wanted to know how I got on with my colleagues.*
> I hope you said the right thing there. What else?
> Well, *they wanted to know how I heard about the job.*
> Did they? Anything else?
> Well, *they wanted to know how much I earned in my present job.*
> Well you certainly had a searching interview—I hope you get the job after all that.

Drill 2: Yes why . . . ? (*Tape section 26/2*)

For practice in converting indirect questions to direct questions. Insist on correct stress.

Tapescript:

You are talking to your colleague after this interview. You are also interested to know the answers to the questions which the interviewer put to him. Listen to these examples:

> He asked me why I was looking for a new job.
> *Yes*, why are *you looking for a new job?*
> And he wanted to know what qualifications I had.
> *Yes*, what qualifications do *you have?*

Notice that the stress is on the first part of the verb. Repeat those questions again.

> *Yes*, why are *you looking for a new job?*
> *Yes*, what qualifications do *you have?*

Now you go on in the same way:

> And he also wanted to know what I liked most about my present job.
> *Yes*, what do *you like most about your present job?*
> And what I liked least about it.
> *Yes*, what do *you like least about it?*
> And he asked me where I studied.
> *Yes*, where did *you study?*
> And how I got on with the management.
> *Yes*, how do *you get on with the management?*
> And how I heard about the job.
> *Yes*, how did *you hear about the job?*
> And, of course, how much I earned.
> *Yes*, how much do *you earn?*
> I don't think that's anything to do with you really!

11 Two reports

Reading and note-taking exercise. Discuss the disparity between the two reports after students have read their respective reports. Reported speech should arise naturally: *He told me . . .*, etc.

12 What really happened? (*Tape section 27*)

Listening and note-taking exercise. Students should only listen out for the information required. There is no need to consider the text in detail.

13 Discussion points

These points can be discussed formally (eg debating style) or used as a springboard for general discussion. A good class could be asked to write a short essay (about 200—300 words) on one of the topics.

12 What do you think?

1 🎧 The public opinion survey (Tape section 28)

There is some room for manoeuvre in ticking the boxes; eg 'Policemen should always carry guns'. The interviewee answers the question equivocally. This could lead on to a discussion of the value of this style of questionnaire in which the interviewee only has a limited range of alternatives.

2 👍 Asking for opinions; giving opinions

For students' reference.

3 👥 What about you?

Students work in pairs for the first part of the exercise. They then ask around the class to find out other students' opinions. Check they are using the language presented in step 2.

4 📖 What they think

Ask questions on the passage to check comprehension and fluency.

5 👍 Making generalizations

There are, of course, other possible exponents—elicit from the class any alternatives and encourage students to add to the list.

6 ✏️ Survey results

Some students will be able to write a cogently argued interpretation of these figures. Others will use the exercise as a controlled practice of exponents which have been taught. There is no reason why the whole class should approach the exercise in the same way.
Students' paragraphs should be like the following:

Most people think that Britain should remain a nuclear power. Nearly 75% disagreed with the statement that Britain should give up all nuclear arms. Opinion was much more divided about worker representaion. Only 31% agreed with the proposal that workers should be represented on boards of directors. And 25% said they 'didn't know', so no clear conclusions can be drawn.

7 🎧 Next item on the agenda (Tape section 29)

Listening and note-taking exercise. Answers as follows:

1. Agenda item: *Recommendations of Working Party on Computerization and Discussion*
2. Matter to be discussed: *Whether to computerize the payroll at the same time as the accounts and stock control system*
3. Advantages of present system: *Works well; can take into account all sorts of little things; flexibility*
4. Result of vote: *In favour of full computerization*

8 👍 Making your point at meetings

This is not a definitive list of exponents—encourage students to suggest others.

9 👥 Putting forward your own ideas

Allow maximum freedom of expression. Refer students to step 2.

10 🎧 Drill 1: What do they think? (Tape section 30/1)

Students use the notes to respond with: *Most people think that . . . should/shouldn't . . .*

Tapescript:

Look at the questionnaire results and then answer the questions. Like this. Listen:

What do most people think about police carrying guns?
Most people think that the police shouldn't carry guns.

I see, and what do the majority think about Britain and the Common Market?
Most people think that Britain shouldn't leave the Common Market.

Now you go on in the same way:

Oh well. That's good news for Europe. What about the monarchy? What's the general opinion there?
Most people think that the monarchy shouldn't be abolished.
And worker participation? What's the majority view?
Most people think that workers shouldn't be represented on the boards of directors.
Then you asked about federalism, didn't you? What did you find there?
Most people think that the UK should be a federal state.
And what did people think about introducing the metric system?
Most people think that the metric system should be introduced in the UK.
And do they think that driving on the right is a good idea?
Most people think that Britain shouldn't drive on the right.
And the last question on your list was about health care and whether it should be free. What do people think about that?
Most people think that health care should be free.

🎧 Drill 2: Sorry to interrupt... (*Tape section 30/2*)

To practise interrupting to ask for clarification. Each time students respond with: *Sorry to interrupt, but what do you mean by...?*

Tapescript:

Listen to this person speaking. Occasionally he uses difficult words. When you do not understand a difficult word or phrase, interrupt and ask for an explanation. Like this. Listen:

And, of course, there's the problem of teething troubles.
Sorry to interrupt, but what do you mean by 'teething troubles'?

I mean the problems associated with introducing the interface technology.
Sorry to interrupt, but what do you mean by 'interface technology'?

Now you go on in the same way:

I mean the machinery and software used by the operator at the visual display unit.
Sorry to interrupt, but what do you mean by 'visual display unit'?
I mean the television monitor which shows information stored in the retrieval system.
Sorry to interrupt, but what do you mean by 'retrieval system'?
I mean any system which is used to store information for later use. Now, as I was saying, we're going to have a lot of problems at the beginning, especially from the point of view of programme development.
Sorry to interrupt, but what do you mean by 'programme development'?
I mean working out the programme which will be fed into the computer. And it's for this reason that I suggest appointing a systems analyst.
Sorry to interrupt, but what do you mean by 'a systems analyst'?
I mean a man who is trained in setting up computer programmes and who understands everything about electronic microprocessors.
Sorry to interrupt, but what do you mean by 'electronic microprocessors'?
I mean the silicon chips which actually store the information inside the computer. So, as I said, apart from the initial teething troubles....
Sorry to interrupt, but what do you mean by 'teething troubles'?
You're not listening, are you?

11 🎭 Two sides to the question

The two teams should meet separately, read through their notes and add any other ideas they can think of to support their views. Then teams meet and try to reach agreements. A definite decision about the future of the PCD need not necessarily be reached.

Optional follow-up writing exercise: memo to the Board of Directors about the future of the PCD.

13 The customer is always right

1 🎞 A dissatisfied customer (*Tape section 31*)

Listening and note-taking practice. The information required is:

Customer's name and address	Global Motors (Mr Brown), Global House, Barn Road, Birmingham 24
Details of order	Item: ABS 1200 Number ordered: 700 Date ordered: 12 June Order number: PQ 1046
Details of delivery	Delivery date: 5 July Invoice date: 29 June Invoice number: A 294351
Details of complaint	High failure rate
Action taken	Credit note for 500 × ABS 1200 = £14,375 Order 700 × ABS 120

2 ✍ Tenses

For controlled practice in the present perfect and simple past tenses. This can be oral or written. The completed passage is as follows:

I'm ringing about a consignment of roller bearings you sent *us about three weeks ago. We* built *them into our Global 2000 model and we* have had *rather a high failure rate on our test run. We've* used *your bearing systems for ten years now and this* has never *happened* before. *And it's nothing to do with the way they were assembled. We've* already *checked* that. *In fact we* checked *the whole production line last Tuesday.*

3 ✍ Dealing with a complaint

The exponents of the various elements of complaints are not definitive—elicit variations from students where possible.

4 👥 Promises

Oral practice in the simple future tense. Students should make up sentences like the following:

1 *I'll prepare it and send it off at once.*
2 *I'll inform them immediately.*
3 *I'll do my best to make sure it doesn't.*
4 *I'll make a note of it now.*
5 *I'll try to be on time.*
6 *I'll make sure it's done for you.*

They could then write up the sentences for homework.

5 👥 Offers

Students should offer help, with sentences like the following:

1 *Would you like me to take you in the car?*
2 *Shall I send you one of our brochures?*
3 *Would you like me to lend you some?*
4 *Shall I explain it to you?*
5 *Would you like me to do it?*
6 *Shall I translate it for you?*

6 👥 Making a complaint

Students recreate conversations as controlled practice. These can be recorded and compared.

7 🎧 Drill 1: Don't worry (*Tape section 32/1*)

For practice in the use of the simple future tense.

Tapescript:

Somebody is ringing to complain about the service given by your company. Promise to do everything you can to help him. Like this. Listen:

I'm very concerned about the delay in sending the goods.
Don't worry. We'll send the goods as soon as possible.
And we've been waiting for ten days for you to forward the operating instructions.
Don't worry. We'll forward the operating instructions as soon as possible.

Now you go on in the same way:

> And another thing. You haven't informed the insurance company about the loss.
> *Don't worry. We'll inform the insurance company about the loss as soon as possible.*
> And I can't understand why you haven't replaced the damaged goods.
> *Don't worry. We'll replace the damaged goods as soon as possible.*
> And what about the spare parts? You haven't dispatched them yet.
> *Don't worry. We'll dispatch them as soon as possible.*
> And you've forgotten to confirm our order.
> *Don't worry. We'll confirm your order as soon as possible.*
> Oh, and there's another thing. You still haven't corrected the invoice.
> *Don't worry. We'll correct the invoice as soon as possible.*
> Yes, and you haven't even sent us a letter of apology for all your mistakes.
> *Don't worry. We'll send a letter of apology as soon as possible.*
> Well, if you don't, I must warn you that we're seriously thinking of taking our business elsewhere.

Drill 2: Can I help? *(Tape section 32/2)*

Students practise offering help, responding each time with: *Would you like me to . . . for you?*

Tapescript:

Your friend is having difficulty in carrying out certain tasks. You offer to help. Listen:

> I've been trying to phone him for half an hour but I can't get through.
> *Would you like me to phone him for you?*
> And I've been trying to translate this report for two hours and I can't make head nor tail of it.
> *Would you like me to translate it for you?*

Now you go on in the same way:

> And I've made so many mistakes typing this report.
> *Would you like me to type it for you?*
> I've been trying to repair this photocopier for ages.
> *Would you like me to repair it for you?*
> And this letter. I've been having great difficulty writing it.
> *Would you like me to write it for you?*
> Thank you. I'm having problems organizing the conference.
> *Would you like me to organize it for you?*
> Oh that would be most kind. And I'm not sure about the agenda. I'm finding it rather difficult to draw up.
> *Would you like me to draw it up for you?*
> Oh, thank you. And there's one more thing. I just don't think I'm going to have time to post this letter.
> *Would you like me to post it for you?*
> Thanks a lot. You're most helpful.

8 Too much noise!

Since this letter forms the basis of the following role play, make sure students understand it.

9 A conflict of interest

Roles can be allocated for the simulation as follows:
   Rollerco management and union representatives;
   Ambermold management;
   Local residents' association;
   Local council representative;
   Noise experts.

The meeting takes place at Rollerco. Ambermold/Rollerco should be as belligerent as possible, insisting that production levels must be maintained in order to meet important export delivery dates.

The noise investigator has suggestions as to how noise levels could be reduced but they would cost £50,000 to implement. Some weekend working could be introduced to set off reduction in night-time working.

Local people are adamant that night-time noise is absolutely unacceptable.

10 A conflict resolved

Remind students of the simple future tense to make promises.

14 A new appointment

1 ▭ The man for the job (*Tape section 33*)

Listening and note-taking exercise. In a weaker class the teacher could provide the information for the duties column and discuss with the class what the requirements might be. The students would then compare those given in the dialogue with their own ideas.

The answers are:

	Requirements	*Duties*
Qualifications	degree in engineering post-grad. diploma in design engineering	to work on new product range
Experience	10–12 years on design problems of precision equipment familiar with COBOL and FORTRAN	to work on his own to be able to use our computers
Age range	35–40	to lead a team of junior engineers
Personal qualities	high motivation creativity eye for detail	to work on own initiative to initiate projects to supervise each step of design phase
Languages	English/French/one other European language	to take over R & D at French plant eventually

2 ◪ Placing emphasis

Point out the importance of correct stress and rhythm in this type of sentence. The new information, which comes after the verb *to be*, is given more emphasis and spoken more slowly than the beginning of the sentence.

3 ♟♟ Practice

Students should refer back to their notes on the dialogue; *enough to* is not a specific teaching point but may need some explanation. The exercise could be extended to requirements for other jobs, including the students' own.

Students should use sentences like the following:

1 *What we're looking for is someone mature enough to lead a team.*
2 *What we need is someone skilled enough to work on his own.*
3 *What we need is someone experienced enough to lead a team of junior engineers.*
4 *What we need is someone fluent enough in French to take over the R & D department at the French plant.*
5 *What we're after is someone creative enough to initiate projects.*

4 ◪ Asking for clarification

Point out that the stress must fall on the words that are being queried: '*How old* did you say he should be?'

5 Abbreviations

A competitive element could be introduced. Which pair can get the most correct answers within a time limit? Spelling should be checked.

6 Be more specific

Point out that in this type of question, *exactly* can follow *where, when, who* or *why* but should precede *how often* or *how many*, etc. The use of *just* before the question word often implies disbelief.

7 Tell me more

Pair work. Check that students use appropriate telephone language to introduce themselves and explain the reason for their call. The telex could then be rewritten with all the necessary details. Students should use sentences like the following:

Who exactly is the telex addressed to?
Just how many have you received?
Exactly how many more do you want?
Which office should we send them to?
Could you be more specific about the problems you have had?
Which of our components has given trouble?
What exactly do you want us to do?
When exactly are you arriving in London?
Who do you want to have talks with?

8 The job advertisement

If English language newspapers are available, look for job advertisements, compare their use of adjectives and discuss the way they create an image of the company and the job.

Students should write advertisements like the following:

International Pharmaceutical Company requires well qualified, creative design engineer to initiate and supervise design of new product range. Fluent French and one other European language desirable. Age range 35–40 with a minimum of 10 years' relevant experience. Excellent pay and conditions.

9 Letter of application

Could be a homework exercise. If relevant to the students' needs, they could write a personal letter to apply for a job for which they are qualified.

10 Drill 1: Yes, but . . . *(Tape section 34/1)*

For practice in placing emphasis. Students respond using notes in their books.

Tapescript:

You are interviewing a candidate who does not appear to have the right qualifications for the job. Listen to these examples:

I speak fluent Russian and Japanese.
Yes, but what we need is someone who can speak French.
And I have three years' experience.
Yes, but what we need is someone with at least 10 years' experience.

Now you go on in the same way. The notes in your book show what sort of person you need for the job.

I'm 25 years old.
Yes, but what we need is someone over 30.
I have two years' marketing experience.
Yes, but what we need is someone with research experience.
And I've got a diploma in accountancy.
Yes, but what we need is someone with an engineering degree.
I enjoy working alone.
Yes, but what we need is someone who can work in a team.
I have always worked in Britain.
Yes, but what we need is someone who has worked overseas.
I'd prefer not to travel too much.
Yes, but what we need is someone who is willing to travel extensively.

Drill 2: Sorry, but . . . *(Tape section 34/2)*

For practice in asking for clarification, students in each case responding with: *Sorry, but what exactly does . . . stand for?*

Tapescript:

During the interview you need to ask the meaning of certain abbreviations. Listen to these examples:

And as you see from my letter, I have an MA in Business Administration.
Sorry, but what exactly does MA stand for?
Master of Arts. And after leaving university I worked for a year in Nigeria with the VSO.
Sorry, but what exactly does VSO stand for?

Now you go on in the same way:

Voluntary Service Overseas—they send volunteers to work all over the world. Anyway I then got a job

in London doing research for a VIP in a large organization.
Sorry, but what exactly does VIP stand for?
Very important person. Head of Planning at the CBI actually.
Sorry, but what exactly does CBI stand for?
Confederation of British Industry. One of my duties was to analyse fluctuations in the FT shares index.
Sorry, but what exactly does FT stand for?
The Financial Times. The index shows the trend of shares sold on the stock exchange. I also had to liaise with the TUC.
Sorry, but what exactly does TUC stand for?
Trades Union Congress—an umbrella organization of all British trade unions. I got married during my time there. My wife was actually MP for West Broomfield.
Sorry, but what exactly does MP stand for?
Member of Parliament. Anyway she lost her seat in the last election and I left the CBI to do market research for ITN . . .

11 The interview

This needs a fairly large room, so that the three candidates can be interviewed simultaneously by the three members of the board. Time should be limited: 10 minutes for the coordination meeting/CV writing, five minutes with each member of the selection board.

Interviewers should each deal with one aspect of the interview—qualifications, previous work experience, personal attitudes, description of the job and conditions of work, salary, etc. Roles could be assigned: personnel manager, head of R and D, production manager. Candidates should invent details for their CV to avoid any feeling of personal failure if not selected. Encourage them to ask questions during the interview. One or two candidates could invent entirely irrelevant qualifications and experience, or demand and try to justify an exhorbitant salary!

Candidates must rotate at the same time to avoid waiting. The teacher or a student, if there are odd numbers, could take the role of secretary, ushering the candidates from one interview to the next. To prevent the candidates waiting passively for a decision from the board, the group could come together and each interviewer give his opinion without consultation. The group as a whole can then decide who gets the job.

15 What would you suggest?

1 A neighbour's advice (*Tape section 35*)

Students first read the introductory paragraph. Ask them to guess what sort of advice Mrs Jamieson will give. Introduce the concept of certainty and uncertainty about advice: *Are you sure?*, etc.

Play the tape at least twice—once for the advice and a second time to decide how certain her advice is. You may wish to play it first to encourage students to guess the meaning of unknown vocabulary, such as *out of the blue, nest egg, safe as houses*, etc.

2 More advice

Pair work. One of each pair is to read the letter, the other the suggestions of Cedric's colleagues. As before, students should note down the advice and the certainty with which it is expressed.

You may need to pre-teach some of the investment terms used.

3 Reporting advice and suggestions

Help students through the explanations, then practise the forms, like this:

> *I've got a headache.*
> *Why not take an aspirin?*
> *He suggested taking an aspirin.*

Ask students to give advice and report on the advice given, until you have worked through all the examples given in the Student's Book.

4 What did they advise Cedric to do?

Students use the language practised in step 3 to report the advice they read in step 2, exchanging the *Daily Chronicle*'s advice with that of Cedric's colleagues. They should also indicate the certainty of this advice.

5 Giving advice; making suggestions

After practising reporting advice, help students to study the way advice is given (directly) and how certainty/uncertainty and formality/informality are expressed. Practise by setting up different situations and asking individual students for their advice.

6 Can you suggest anything?

After students have practised in pairs (taking it in turns to be visitors to Britain), continue with a class discussion to check students' fluency with the certainty/uncertainty and formal/informal phrases. Allow students to make their own suggestions.

Next students write sentences giving suggestions to foreign visitors to their countries. Encourage them to use the certainty/uncertainty phrases presented in previous steps.

7 Yes or no? (*Tape section 36*)

Note-taking and listening exercise. Check the notes against the tapescript in the Student's Book.

8 Drill 1: What did he say? (*Tape section 37/1*)

Using the notes they made in step 7, students are to respond with:

> *He recommended . . . -ing*, or
> *He advised me not to . . .* , or
> *He advised me not to . . . unless I got professional help.*

It may be necessary to check students' notes before starting the drill.

Tapescript:

You are Cedric. Using the notes you have made, answer your colleague's questions about your talk with the bank manager. Listen to these examples:

> So you've been talking to the bank manager about your plans, Cedric. What did he have to say?
> *Well, he recommended investing in property.*
> Yes, anything else?
> *Well, he advised me not to invest in Krugerrands.*
> Mmm, and what about shares?

Well, he advised me not to invest in shares unless I got professional help.

Now you go on in the same way:

Yes that's probably wise. What about building societies?
Well, he recommended investing in building societies.
And did he say anything about unit trust funds?
Well, he advised me not to invest in unit trust funds unless I got professional help.
I see. Did you mention starting an art collection?
Well, he advised me not to invest in an art collection.
Too risky, I suppose. What else was there?
Well, he advised me not to invest in my own business unless I got professional help.
And what about your crazy idea of the theatre . . . ?
Well, he advised me not to invest in a theatrical production.

Drill 2: What would you advise?
(Tape section 37/2)

In each exchange, students offer both an original suggestion, starting: *Well, I think you should . . .* and an alternative suggestion, starting: *Well, you could always . . .* Original and alternative suggestions are given in the Student's Book.

Tapescript:

You work for an advertising agency. A discussion with one of your clients is in progress. He is not impressed with your original ideas so you put forward a more conventional solution. Look at the notes in your book and listen to these examples:

Now what would you advise for our new brand of cigarettes?
Well, I think you should hire a plane to write the brand name across the sky.
Oh no, that wouldn't reach a wide enough audience.
Well, you could always take out a large advertisement in a national paper.
Mmm, maybe, and what about our cigarette lighter campaign?
Well, I think you should scatter thousands of leaflets over London from helicopters.
I'm sure that's against the law.
Well, you could always try a direct mail shot.

Now you go on in the same way.

And then there's our new low priced cigarette range.
Well, I think you should recruit private car owners to advertise on their cars.
Oh, I don't think that would work.
Well, you could always launch a poster campaign.

Yes, and what ideas do you have for our exclusive multi-coloured cigarettes?
Well, I think you should give a champagne reception for VIPs at next month's International Fair.
I don't think that would give us enough publicity.
Well, you could always distribute free samples.

And our slim-line cigars. What do you advise for that?
Well, I think you should get the film star Mimi La Tour to advertise them on TV.
Oh no, she doesn't project the right image at all.
Well, you could always advertise on Commercial Radio.

And finally our 'Outdoor Man' pipe tobacco.
Well, I think you should sponsor a formula one racing car.
Oh no, far too expensive—and risky.
Well, you could always take your account to another agency!

9 Cedric's dilemma

Investment information could be read and discussed as a class, before dividing into small groups. Recap on all advice given so far, and what students know of Cedric as a person.

After each group has made its recommendations discuss what investments are possible and most profitable in the students' own country/countries.

16 Weighing it up

1 A flat in London

Note-taking and reading exercise. Vocabulary relating to housing could be discussed and pre-taught. The distance from Piccadilly could be compared from a number of different underground stations.

2 Differences and similarities

Phrases presented for students' reference. Ask individual students to compare other things for extra practice if required.

3 Intensifiers

Presentation and exemplification for students' reference.

4 The quotation

Read and discuss the table briefly. Focus on the degree of difference between the three companies' offers. The exercise could be done for homework and the answers compared in class. Note that *somewhat* and *slightly* are interchangeable.

For further writing practice students could make a similar report on the three quotations for fluorescent tubes in Unit 3.

The complete report is as follows:

While British Bearings' quotation for supplying the parts required for CX135 is slightly *lower than Aluco's, the quality of the steel is* definitely *inferior. Similarly, their delivery dates are* not nearly *so satisfactory. Aluco seem to be a* far *more* efficient *company altogether. Furthermore, Aluco has an* incomparably *wider range, and their UK market share was* roughly *the same as Ambermold's last year, although they are somewhat* less well-known *abroad. There appears to be no* great *difference between the offers of Aluco and Ambermold. The prices quoted are more or less the same, and their delivery dates too are almost identical. I think we can definitely exclude British Bearings but should give a good deal more thought to both Ambermold and Aluco.*

5 Regents Park, Hampstead or Maida Vale?

The sentences could be done orally, then in writing. Make sure students use intensifiers and the comparative forms presented above.

Further discussion points could be a comparison of property prices in students' own countries, housing policies, what makes a 'desirable residential area', etc.

Model sentences:

From the point of view of size, there's no comparison between the studio and the Hampstead flat.
From the point of view of cost, renting the Maida Vale flat would be considerably cheaper than buying a flat.
From the point of view of distance, there's very little to choose between Hampstead and Maida Vale.

6 Decision making (Tape section 38)

Listening and note-taking exercise. Ask individual students if they agree with the recommendations made.
Students should note down the following:

	Algiers	Dubai	London
Number of visits per year	18	20	25
Average length of stay	10 days	18 days	1 week
Average monthly rent for a flat	£400	£1,000	£300–£400
Average price of a two-bedroom flat	—	—	£100,000
Recommendation	hotel	rent	buy

7 Preferences

Focus on the use of the simple past tense after *I'd rather* and *I'd sooner*. Introduce short answers, such as *I'd rather not* and *I prefer not to*.

8 On the whole I'd rather ...

If you wish, start the step with oral pair work or class discussion. Students then write up the sentences at home.

9 Telex

Students' telex should be like the following:

CONSIDERING BUYING APARTMENT LONDON FOR USE OF VISITING COMPANY EMPLOYEES. KINDLY MAKE INITIAL ENQUIRIES RE FORMALITIES, PRICE RANGE, AVAILABILITY. HERMAN KAUFMANN ARRIVING LONDON 22 MARCH TO MAKE FINAL SELECTION. BEST REGARDS.

10 Drill 1: You or me? *(Tape section 39/1)*

Students respond with: *No, actually I'd rather you ...* (simple past) or *No, actually I'd rather ...* (infinitive) *myself*.

Tapescript:

Your secretary is checking the jobs to be done while you are away from the office. Some of them you would rather do yourself. Listen to these examples:

Now you wanted to make an appointment with Mr Smith. Do you want to make that yourself?
No, actually I'd rather you made it.
And what about the telex from the London office. Shall I reply to it?
No, actually I'd rather reply to it myself.

Now you go on in the same way. Your secretary is always wrong about who should do the jobs.

And what about the arrangements for next month's trade fair. Are you going to make them?
No, actually I'd rather you made them.
And someone will have to interview the applicants for the typing pool. I suppose you'll do that yourself.
No, actually I'd rather you interviewed them.
And would you like me to draw up the agenda for the meeting on Thursday?
No, actually I'd rather draw it up myself.
OK. And the cocktail party on Wednesday—will you write the invitation?
No, actually I'd rather you wrote them.
As you wish. And don't forget your wife's birthday on Tuesday. You'll order the flowers, I suppose?
No, actually I'd rather you ordered them.

Drill 2: Yes, but ... *(Tape section 39/2)*

Students respond with the aid of the notes in their books, starting each time: *Yes, but on balance I think it's worth doing to....*

Tapescript:

After a discussion on changes to be made in the office, you have this conversation with your secretary. Listen to these examples:

You realize that most of these changes will mean a great deal more expense.
Yes, but on balance I think it's worth doing to improve efficiency.
For example, you want to change the invoicing system. We'll need at least three more office staff.
Yes, but on balance I think it's worth doing to simplify our records.

Now you go on in the same way. Give reasons for your decisions. The notes will help you.

And you really think we should buy another photocopier? The old one still works perfectly.
Yes, but on balance I think it's worth doing to save time.
You want to set up an in-house magazine. It'll take a lot of time and effort.
Yes, but on balance I think it's worth doing to improve internal communication.
You also really feel we should hold weekly meetings in all departments. It'll take up so much time.
Yes, but on balance I think it's worth doing to encourage more team spirit.
And installing word processors in the typing pool. We've managed without them quite satisfactorily so far.
Yes, but on balance I think it's worth doing to speed up order processing.
And you want to set up a customer service department to deal with complaints. More staff needed—and another office.
Yes, but on balance I think it's worth doing to create goodwill.
And you're in favour of appointing Mr Jeffries as head of the new advertising department. He's almost 60 years old— and not in very good health.
Yes, but on balance I think it's worth doing to counteract the inexperience of the rest of the team.
Well, I suppose your ideas are worth trying!

11 Siting a factory

Students could be asked to invent further details about each site. In particular no information is given about the proximity of components suppliers, other industry in the area, climate, housing. The six place names are imaginary.

12 A report

Students are to report the decisions made in step 11 and the reasons for them, using the language presented in steps 2, 3 and 7.

17 Better than ever

1 ▣ Presenting the product (Tape section 40)

Listening and note-taking exercise. Some vocabulary may need to be pre-taught: *analgesic, soluble, ingredient, swallow*. The topic of drug safety, particularly with regard to children, should be introduced.

Answers:
1 What has been changed?
   The taste of the undissolved tablets is bitter.
   The container has been made child-resistant.
   The labelling and instructions are clearer.
   The price is higher.
2 What is the purpose of the changes?
   To discourage children from thinking of the tablets as sweets.
   To make the containers difficult for a child to open.
   To make the instructions easier for mothers to understand.
   To cover the cost of research.
3 What has not been changed?
   The active ingredients.
   The speed with which the tablets act.
   The taste of the tablets dissolved in water.

2 ✍ Presentation techniques

Most of these points have appeared in previous units. In this unit the aim is to give students practice in using them to convey a message effectively. The tape (tape section 40) could be played again after going through this section to focus on the way these forms are used.

3 ✎ Welcome to the company

Students should rewrite the text as follows:

> May I begin by welcoming you all to Fittenwell Pharmaceuticals.
> Perhaps I could start by giving you an outline of the company's history.
> I'd like to move on now to a brief explanation of our management structure.
> And now we come to the most important point—what we expect from our employees.
> And finally I'd like to hand you over to our personnel manager for a tour of the building.

4 ✎ We can help

This can be a homework exercise. Using the language from step 2, students should produce the following sentences:

1 *Shortlisting candidates for interview is the most time-consuming task for a personnel department.*
2 *What you need is a reliable agency to relieve the pressure of routine recruitment.*
3 *All your recruitment problems can be solved by our agency.*
4 *Only the most suitable applicants are passed on to you for interview.*
5 *Never have we failed to satisfy our customers' requirements.*
6 *We do understand your needs.*

5 ▣ Any questions? (Tape section 41)

Listening comprehension. Students should read the worksheet through carefully before listening to the tape. The first two statements are false; the next two are both true, the fifth is false and the last is true.

6 ✍ A good question

After reading through this section, tape section 41 could be played again to focus attention on how points are raised and how the speaker deals with them.

7 ♟♟ Make your point

Students should produce sentences like the following:

1 *You said that we must make a distinction between urban and rural areas. Could you tell us why this is necessary?*
2 *Earlier in your speech you said that public transport is as essential as water and electricity supplies. Later you mentioned the fact that most families today own cars. If this is true, surely public transport is no longer essential?*
3 *Could I go back to your statement about government subsidies? Do you really think the tax payers would agree to this?*
4 *On the subject of private cars, you stated that these*

should be banned from inner cities. Do you really consider this possible unless public transport is first made more efficient?

5 *I'd like to go back to your statement that public transport cannot be a profit-making operation. This is not in fact the case. Many private rail and bus companies exist, and they must make a profit...*

These points can be prepared for homework and, instead of pair work, you could ask one or two students to make the statements and the rest of the class to respond with their points.

8 Fittenwell on the spot

Pair work. If a tape recorder is available, students could record their dialogue. Parts of the taped version could then be replayed in class to illustrate effective use of the language presented, and for correction.

9 Visual aids

Useful language for presenting visual aids at a lecture or demonstration.

10 A new approach to order processing

Weaker groups need only write six sentences; advanced classes could expand the notes further—see below. The correct use of the article and prepositions may need revision before an exercise where notes have to be expanded to full sentences.

> *As you can see from this flow chart the present system consists of six separate stages. This next flow chart illustrates the proposed new system which has only three stages. The advantages of the new system are speed, efficiency and a reduction in manpower. It has been said that the new system might increase the workload in the order processing department and the possibility of errors being made. We have therefore come up with two proposals to overcome these objections. First a salary review for the staff concerned, which this diagram illustrates. Secondly the appointment of an 'order processing controller'. Finally, I should just like to say that the new system works. This graph shows the increase in orders in a rival company since they started using a system similar to the one we propose.*

11 Drill 1: You mentioned... *(Tape section 42/1)*

Using the jumbled notes in their books, students respond with: *Yes, you mentioned..., but I see here that...*

Tapescript:

There are discrepancies between the salesman's claims and the information in the catalogue. Listen to these examples:

> Now are there any questions about operating the machine?
> *Yes, you mentioned ease of operation, but I see here that there are forty pages of operating instructions.*
> Yes, but I think you'll find it is really quite simple. Now any queries about the material?
> *Yes, you mentioned lightweight material, but I see here that it weighs thirty kilos.*

Now you go on in the same way. The notes show the speaker's claims about the machine and the information from the sales catalogue.

> Well, for a machine this size that's quite reasonable. Any questions about delivery?
> *Yes, you mentioned prompt delivery, but I see here that the delivery period is six months.*
> That was last year. It's reduced to eight weeks now. Any queries about the price?
> *Yes, you mentioned a low price, but I see here that it costs £25,000.*
> Well, that is relatively low, you know. And you realize, I suppose, that the machine has a tremendously long working life.
> *Yes, you mentioned above average durability, but I see here that it's guaranteed for 18 months.*
> Yes, well, we're considering extending that to two years and of course I explained that customers are offered a servicing contract.
> *Yes, you mentioned an inexpensive servicing contract, but I see here that it costs £500 a year.*
> Yes, but that includes all parts and labour. Have you any other questions about maintenance?
> *Yes, you mentioned trouble free maintenance, but I see here that it needs servicing every four weeks.*
> Yes, but we are being rather over-cautious there.

Drill 2: Yes, but... *(Tape section 42/2)*

In each case students respond with the opposite of the cue-word *high* or *low*, beginning: *Yes, I take your point, but this graph shows how high/low... are this year.*

Tapescript:

The manager of one of Fittenwell's divisions has been presenting last year's figures. He accepts the directors' criticism of his division's poor results last year. Fortunately he can show that the situation is much better this year.

> These figures are appalling. Your overseas sales were the lowest in the group last year.
> *Yes, I take your point, but this graph shows how high overseas sales are this year.*
> And you must reduce costs. Your production costs

were far too high last year.
Yes, I take your point, but this graph shows how low production costs are this year.

Now you go on in the same way. Remember to stress the important words: *low* or *high* and *this year*.

And your annual turnover must be improved. It was the lowest in the company.
Yes, I take your point, but this graph shows how high the annual turnover is this year.
And in the home market—most disappointing. Home market sales were lower than any previous year.
Yes, I take your point, but this graph shows how high home market sales are this year.
And your workforce! Last year you had the highest absenteeism ever. This must improve.
Yes, I take your point, but this graph shows how low absenteeism is this year.
And of course there's been a corresponding decrease in production. Your productivity is far too low.
Yes, I take your point, but this graph shows how high productivity is this year.
And the question of pay. The wage rises you gave everyone were far too high.
Yes, I take your point, but this graph shows how low wage rises are this year.
And your expenditure. It must be cut. You spent far too much on overheads last year.
Yes, I take your point, but this graph shows how low overheads are this year.

12 Take the floor

Alternatively, a few students could take the floor at the beginning or end of each class period for a week or so. Students should keep strictly to the time limit, and everyone be encouraged to participate in the question and answer session.

18 Consolidation exercises

Use either as progress tests or remedial exercises. Points tested are covered in Units 10 to 17. The key gives model answers to open-ended exercises.

The background situation, the development of a replacement for the ZB series, could be developed into a full role play, if required.

KEY

1 Appointments

On Monday *I'm having* a meeting with the Metalco Directors, starting at 10.30. *We're stopping* for lunch at 13.00 and *starting* again at 14.30. *We're discussing* the manufacture of the ZB 11 under licence. On Tuesday Mr Jacques *is coming* to see us. *He's arriving* at 11.00 and then *I'm showing* him round the factory from 11.30 to 13.00. In the afternoon *we're negotiating* the terms of the agency agreement, *starting* at 14.00. On Wednesday *I'm reporting* to the Board on all the current projects in the morning at 10.00 and *visiting* the Leeds factory in the afternoon. On Thursday morning *I'm preparing* production statistics for the accounts department and at 2.15 *we're having* a meeting to discuss the development of a new range to replace the ZB.

2 Redesign

If we stop production of the ZB range next year, our customers *will* complain.
If we close the Leeds factory temporarily, the unions *will* take industrial action.
If we spend £150,000 on designing a replacement, other projects *could* suffer.
If we tell the press of our plans, shares *might* fall.
If we ask the bank to finance the project, they *will* charge extremely high rates of interest.
If we submit the plan to the Board before all the details are finalized, they *will* reject it.
If we buy cheaper components, quality and reliability *may* be a problem.

3 Minutes

At the meeting between the Project Coordination Department and the Research and Development Team held on 24 September at 2.30 pm, Peter Elton *explained* that the ZB range was out of date and that sales had been falling steadily. He *said* that customers were turning to competitors, eg Corbridge Electronics. He *asked* if it was worth spending money marketing an unsuccessful product.

David Young *asked* Peter Elton if he had any statistics to support these statements. He *wanted to know* which customers we were losing.

Elton *replied* that the total sales of the ZB range had fallen by 17% during the previous six months, and he *mentioned* that Birtley's were dissatisfied with the ZB.

Miss Winter *asked* if it wouldn't be better to develop the new product range before we stopped production of the ZB.

Elton *answered* by saying that we already had large stocks, enough for nine months. In that time we could develop a prototype of the replacement.

4 Complaints

The missing words, in order, are: *regret, satisfied, component, appreciate, reputation, manufacturers, supply, technology, alternative*.

5 Clarification

1 *Exactly how many* of your customers have complained?
2 *Exactly how long* have you used the ZB range?
3 *What exactly do you mean* by 'no longer suitable'?
4 *Just who* can supply a better component?
5 What does FIDM *stand for*?
6 *When exactly* did you send another letter of complaint?
7 *Who exactly* is responsible for your final decision?

6 Suggestions

Having considered proposals to stop production of the ZB range and replace it with a new product, we would make the following comments:

We think it would be a good idea to carry out a small-scale feasibility study first, and at the same time ask existing customers for their comments on a modernized ZB range.

We would suggest that you continue production of the ZB meanwhile.

We would also advise you to consult staff. The Union should be fully informed and assured that no jobs are at risk and production engineers should be sent on training courses immediately. *We also feel it would be advisable to* approach the bank *now* for help with finance next year.

Finally, in order to ensure continuity, *we suggest that* you keep the name ZB rather than give the product a completely new name.

7 Prototype

The questionnaires completed by five companies who have used the ZB Micro in prototype form show very favourable results overall, particularly as far as speed, accuracy and economy are concerned. It seems that the proposed price is considered rather high and the opinion of workmanship and reliability of the ZB is not as high as it might be. Most companies think that the ZB Micro handles reasonably easily, although clearly Global Motors experienced some problems.

19 Expanding overseas

1 📼 Abu Nafat—an expert's view (*Tape section 43*)

Play the tape once, then fill in the worksheet as far as possible in groups or as a class. Play a second time for missing information. Discuss how relevant this information is to the decision they have to take about going into the market in Abu Nafat. The information is:

Topic	Information
Geographical situation	Large peninsula on Arabian Red Sea coast. Excellent natural harbour.
Religion	Islam

History
  early
  1800–1918
  1918–1946
  1946–1965
  1965–now
	
	Inhabited 4000 BC, 7th century converted to Islam.
	Part of Ottoman Empire.
	Pro-British Monarchy installed.
	Army coup. Republic. Jamil Sultan first President.
	Army coup.

Politics
  1965–today
 	
  political alignment
  political stability
  future plans
	
	Non-aligned. Takes firm line with Western companies and governments.
	Member of non-aligned group.
	Good. No organized opposition.
	New constitution; election of National Assembly.

The economy today
  oil
  other industry
  financial standing
	
	Abu Nafat National Oil Company controls 51% of oil industry.
	Petrochemicals, steel, agriculture.
	Good.

2 ✏️ Past tenses

These have been taught in previous units and are presented together here for general revision and practice.

3 ✏️ Which tense?

Could be homework or individual written exercises. Errors will show if further revision is needed. Answers are:

1. *have been*
2. *have been working*
3. *have discovered*
4. *were working*
5. *found*
6. *arrived*
7. *had explored*
8. *had had*
9. *were classified*
10. *(were) taken*
11. *has just given*
12. *opened*
13. *has increased*
14. *were digging*
15. *unearthed*
16. *decided*

4 The passive

The present and present perfect passive is introduced and practised in Unit 8 with reference to describing a process. Here more general applications are presented.

5 Achievements and projects

A written or oral exercise. Focus on the need for the passive form to be used, since the subject in each case is the Government. Students could make similar brief reports on developments in their home town/country/company. Model sentences:

In 1969 a new steel plant was opened.
Since 1969 priority has been given to investment in industry.
The first international Trade Fair was held in Abu Nafat 10 years ago.
Two hospitals and fifteen new schools have been built in the last five years.
10% of the GNP is now being invested in new industries.
A new six-lane motorway is being constructed.
Next year the second phase of agricultural reform will be completed.
In three years' time new university buildings will be opened.

6 North African projects

Model article:
The financing of a number of projects in North Africa is being discussed by UN economists. An important part of the gas pipeline network has already been financed by international credit markets and it is reported that the central banks of the countries concerned will guarantee the loans. A long term loan for the construction of a dam in the north east has been arranged by the World Bank, and the site is at present being surveyed by World Bank experts.
  Some countries may ask the Food and Agriculture Organization to advise on pest control. If experts were needed, one team would probably be sent to each affected area.
  A symposium on the return of African works of art to national museums is being planned by UNESCO.

7 Expressions of time relating to past events

Check that the meaning of all the time expressions to be used is clear. Point out that the context as well as the structure of the sentence determines which is most appropriate. The missing expressions, in order, are:

1. as far back as
2. not until
3. prior to
4. shortly before
5. during
6. immediately after
7. by the time
8. meanwhile
9. in recent years

8 Drill 1: Yes, we did... (*Tape section 44/1*)

For controlled practice in the present perfect continuous.

Tapescript:

Your company had an excellent record in the seventies, but has not been doing so well recently. Listen to these examples:

  In the seventies your company sold a lot of goods abroad.
  Yes, we did, but latterly we've been having difficulty in selling goods abroad.
  And you also paid very high salaries.
  Yes, we did, but latterly we've been having difficulty in paying high salaries.

Now you go on in the same way.

  And you used to get government contracts.
  Yes, we did, but latterly we've been having difficulty in getting government contracts.
  And you always recruited first class staff.
  Yes, we did, but latterly we've been having difficulty in recruiting first class staff.
  And you brought out new products regularly.
  Yes, we did, but latterly we've been having difficulty in bringing out new products.
  And you managed to keep your prices stable in the seventies.
  Yes, we did, but latterly we've been having difficulty in keeping our prices stable.
  And throughout the seventies you maintained a high level of investment.
  Yes, we did, but latterly we've been having difficulty in maintaining a high level of investment.
  And you always paid high dividends to shareholders.
  Yes, we did, but latterly we've been having difficulty in paying high dividends.
  Well I shouldn't worry too much—everyone else has been having difficulties too!

Drill 2: Right... (*Tape section 44/2*)

For controlled practice of various passive tenses.

Tapescript:

You are making notes on messages to be passed on to your boss when he returns from his holiday. Listen to these examples:

  Now don't forget to tell him that the plumber came and has mended the radiator.
  Right, the radiator has been mended.
  And the new typist—you know the one who can't spell—well she is typing the sales report now.
  Right, the sales report is being typed now.

Now you go on in the same way.

  But with all the extra work we haven't managed to finalize the details on the agency contract, but we

will sign the contract next week.
Right, the contract will be signed next week.
And don't forget to tell him about the goods ordered by IMG that they returned—he left instructions about it and I sent a credit note yesterday.
Right, a credit note was sent yesterday.
And he asked me to put in a claim to the insurance company. Well I haven't quite finished it yet. But tell him that my secretary will post the claim tomorrow morning.
Right, the claim will be posted tomorrow morning.
And you remember he wasn't happy with the packaging—well tell him we've changed it.
Right, the packaging has been changed.
And the catalogue. He wanted me to get it translated into German. Well, it's at the printers' now. I don't know when it will be ready but they are printing it.
Right, the catalogue is being printed.
And finally don't forget to say that the advertising agency phoned last week and quoted a much lower fee for the campaign. They have reduced their estimate by 15 per cent.
Right, the estimate has been reduced by 15 per cent.

9 Strictly between you and me (*Tape section 45*)

Note-taking and listening exercise. On the following topics, the comments expressed are:

1 climate: *negative*
2 social life: *negative*
3 financial returns: *positive*
4 paperwork: *negative:*
5 the president: *negative*
6 political stability: *positive*
7 scenery: *positive*

10 A more acceptable turn of phrase

Listening, vocabulary and register exercise, giving an alternative view of Abu Nafat. Point out that some of the expressions are colloquial and would be unsuitable in very formal situations. The expressions in the dialogue are:

he's very strong-willed: *he's a bit of an autocrat*
the climate is unpleasant: *the climate is foul*
do not particularly like him: *can take him or leave him*
to follow bureaucratic procedures: *to get through all the red tape*
strongly support: *is right behind (him)*
I would go even further: *that's putting it mildly*

11 Decision time

You can ask students to write short memos. Refer them to Unit 18, step 6.

20 Business abroad

1 ▣ Phoning the travel agent (*Tape section 46*)

Remind students of the previous unit and the possibility of Abu Nafat as a potential area for a new sales subsidiary. Check on travel vocabulary.

The travel agent will not be able to give some of the information. Get the students to predict some of the requests Janice Freeman will make. Introduce the notion of requesting and offering. Write down the exponents suggested by the students for later comparison with those used in the conversation and the language summary. In a weak class, half the class could listen for the information requested and half for the travel agent's replies which could then be matched up.

Here is the information requested and given:

frequency of flights: *one direct flight a week*
fares: *no information*
departure and arrival times: *depart 7.30, arrive 17.20*
flights from other cities: *Paris (Thursday), Frankfurt (Saturday, Monday)*
connecting flights: *no information*
return flights: *no information*

2 ✋ Making and responding to offers

Add any alternatives suggested by the students. Discuss the degree of formality and appropriateness in situations they have experienced.

3 ✋ Making and responding to requests

As for step 2. Discuss any differences in the students' choice of order. Point out the exponents that would be suitable in written language. Point out the 'neutral' forms that can be used in almost all circumstances.

4 ♟ Problems

This could be a written or oral exercise, to be done in pairs. Encourage students to develop the dialogues by giving reasons for B's responses. Similar 'free' dialogues could be worked out with students making requests to each other.

5 ♟ Making a phone call

The re-enactment will not follow the taped version exactly, but ensure that all the points are covered and appropriate expressions used.

6 🎭 Special requests

Give the students some time to read the information, check comprehension, but do not encourage them to write out their parts.

7 ⟳ Drill 1: I could if you like . . . (*Tape section 47/1*)

For controlled practice in one form of response to a request for help. Make sure the students' intonation is correct—in particular that they do not give *if you like* undue emphasis.

Tapescript:

The Marketing Manager is busy, so you offer to help him. Listen to these examples:

I need this letter typed.
I could type it if you like.
Someone ought to reply to this enquiry.
I could reply to it if you like.

Now you go on the same way.

This telegram should be sent immediately.
I could send it if you like.
Mr Meyer should be rung today.
I could ring him if you like.
The petty cash should be checked.
I could check it if you like.
And the minutes need to be written up.
I could write them up if you like.
And I must cancel my appointments for tomorrow.
I could cancel them if you like.
And my reservation for the evening's flight needs to be confirmed.
I could confirm it if you like.

Drill 2: Do you think you could...?
(Tape section 47/2)

For controlled practice of one particular form of request. As before, make sure students use the correct intonation.

Tapescript:

You are using your Manchester colleague's office. You need some work done, but you don't know how busy his secretary is, so you ask her politely. Listen to these examples:

> I wonder if she would bring me the Sales Director's report.
> Er..., Miss Haylock, do you think you could possibly bring me the Sales Director's report?
> I wonder if she would type this letter for me.
> Er..., Miss Haylock, do you think you could possibly type this letter for me?

Now you go on in the same way.

> I wonder if she'd make me a cup of coffee.
> Er..., Miss Haylock, do you think you could possibly make me a cup of coffee?
> I wonder if she would send this letter by registered mail for me.
> Er..., Miss Haylock, do you think you could possibly send this letter by registered mail for me?
> I wonder if she'd reserve two seats for the opera tonight.
> Er..., Miss Haylock, do you think you could possibly reserve two seats for the opera tonight?
> I wonder if she'd confirm my return flight to Geneva.
> Er..., Miss Haylock, do you think you could possibly confirm my return flight to Geneva?
> I wonder if she'd copy these papers for me?
> Er..., Miss Haylock, do you think you could possibly copy these papers for me?
> I wonder if she'd answer this telex for me?
> Er..., Miss Haylock, do you think you could possibly answer this telex for me?

8 Negotiations in Abu Nafat

Students skim-read to find these corresponding words and phrases:

total obedience: *strict adherence*
drinking no alcohol: *teetotal*
were caused by: *stemmed from*
principally: *mainly*
in contrast to this: *on the other hand*

Check that both sides are aware of the importance of the fact that the Abu Nafat team want a *manufacturing* not a *sales* subsidiary, as the discussion will really hinge on this. Each side should also realize that agreement is equally important to Fittenwell, because Abu Nafat and the Red Sea is a rich new market, and to Abu Nafat, because it will bring employment and expertise.

In a large class divide into groups of six—three to each side. During the preparation time encourage the teams to agree on where they would be prepared to compromise during the negotiations and to add any further points to the notes given. One of the Abu Nafat team would act as chairman. A useful revision point would be how to welcome visitors and thank hosts for their hospitality. Specific roles could be defined: for Abu Nafat, representatives of the Ministries of Trade, Health and Finance; for Fittenwell, Jonathan Morley, Janice Freeman and a member of the Medical Department.

Written follow-up could take the form of a report from each side (one to the Fittenwell Board of Directors and one to the Minister of Trade) summarizing the negotiations and giving recommendations.

9 Letter writing

This should be presented in class but could then be completed at home.

21 That's what must have happened

1 🎧 An encouraging start (*Tape section 48*)

Listening and note-taking exercise. The answers are:

Was Robert Cave able to:
1 see the Purchasing Manager? *Yes*
2 explain Fittenwell's full range of products? *No*
3 interest Mr Avon in the service provided by Fittenwell? *Yes*
4 find out about their present purchasing arrangements? *Yes*
5 make another appointment? *Yes*
6 obtain a firm order? *No*

2 ✏️ Dialogue

Gap filling. Play the tape again with pauses if necessary. Refer students to the tapescript for correction.

3 📖 Ability and achievement

After reading through this section, go back to the dialogue and discuss what alternatives could be used to fill the gaps. Focus on the fact that while *managed to*, *was able to* and *succeeded in* are all used to express the achievement of an objective, *could* in past affirmative sentences refers only to ability, not achievement.

4 👥 Ups and downs

Start with pair work; then individual writing, which could be done at home. Point out that *could* cannot be used to describe the company's achievements. Students should make their positive statements with *were able to* and their negative statements with *weren't able to* or *couldn't*.

5 👥 A brighter future

Group members should pool ideas and make sentences like these:

Now we'll be able to repair the roof at headquarters.
And we may be able to take back all the men made redundant.
Now we can pay off part of the bank loan.

If necessary, start with a brief introduction. Write suggestions on the board; students then decide how urgent these suggestions are.

6 🎧 What can have happened? (*Tape section 49*)

Listening and note-taking exercise. Answers are:

Robert mistook the date. *Impossible*
Robert mistook the time. *Impossible*
Mr Avon forgot the appointment. *Possible*
Mr Avon was in the office but didn't want to see Robert. *Possible*
The receptionist made a mistake. *Impossible*
Mr Avon was called away on an emergency. *Certain*

7 📖 Did he . . .?

Make sure students appreciate the weak stress on *have*.

8 📖 Who's who?

It is important to mark information from the clues on the grid with √ and ×, so that the solution becomes clear. For example, *The sales visit was to Paris* would provide the following information:

	London	Paris	New York
Trade fair		×	
Sales visit	×	√	×
Language course		×	

An overhead projector is useful to project the grid onto the board and the exercise done as a non-competitive class activity. After reading each clue, fill in all possible √'s and ×'s on the grid. As each box is filled in, students should make complete sentences using *can't/ couldn't have, must have, might have*. From the first clue the following sentences could be made:

The Paris trip must have taken one month.
It can't have lasted 2 days or 5 days.
The New York trip can't have taken one month.
The London visit might have lasted 5 days.
The 2-day trip must have been either to London or to New York.

When all the information from the clues has been transferred to the grid, the blanks in sentences below each clue should be easy to fill in.

Students could make up similar puzzles for the rest of the group. They are fun to write!

The grid and sentences should be completed as follows:

9 Drill 1: When I was sixteen . . .
(Tape section 50/1)

Students use the notes in their books to respond with *Yes, I was able to get that job because I could . . . when I was sixteen.*

Tapescript:

At a job interview a candidate is questioned about her previous experience. Listen to these examples:

I hear you had a great variety of holiday jobs while you were still at school. It's unusual for a girl to get a job as life guard at a swimming pool, isn't it?
Yes, I was able to get that job because I could swim very well when I was sixteen.
And another one was at a horse riding school.
Yes, I was able to get that job because I could ride very well when I was sixteen.

Now you go on in the same way. The notes will help you.

	London	Paris	New York	One month	Five days	Two days	Trade Fair	Sales visit	Language course
Mr Brown	√	×	×	×	×	√	×	√	×
Mr White	×	×	√	×	√	×	√	×	×
Mr Green	×	√	×	√	×	×	×	×	√
Trade Fair	×	×	√	×	√	×			
Sales visit	√	×	×	×	×	√			
Language course	×	√	×	√	×	×			
One month	×	√	×						
Five days	×	×	√						
Two days	√	×	×						

1 *The sales visit* couldn't have been *in Paris.*
   The Trade Fair might have been *in Paris.*
2 So *Mr White* couldn't have gone *on the sales visit,* but *he* might have gone *on a language course or to the Trade Fair.*
3 So *Mr Green* must have gone *to Paris, Mr Brown* must have gone *to London and Mr White* must have gone *to New York.*
4 *Mr Brown's trip was the shortest. He* must have gone *on the sales visit to London.*
   Mr White didn't go on the language course. He must have gone *to the Trade Fair in New York.*
   So *Mr Green* must have gone *to Paris on the language course.*

And then you taught dancing, I believe?
Yes, I was able to get that job because I could dance very well when I was sixteen.
And you were given a part in a musical show one year?
Yes, I was able to get that job because I could sing very well when I was sixteen.
And later you worked in a restaurant.
Yes, I was able to get that job because I could cook very well when I was sixteen.
And another of your jobs, I see, was as a guide to foreign tourists.
Yes, I was able to get that job because I could speak French and German very well when I was sixteen.

And you were also a secretary for a short time.
Yes, I was able to get that job because I could type very well when I was sixteen.
You also worked for a dressmaker.
Yes, I was able to get that job because I could sew very well when I was sixteen.
And can't you do all these things now you're twenty-eight?

🎧 Drill 2: What do you think? (*Tape section 50/2*)

Students use the notes in their books to respond with *Yes, he might have found out about that* . . . or *No, he can't have found out about that.* . . .

Tapescript:

The boss has just sent a message to say that he wishes to speak to you about a very serious matter. With a colleague you try to work out what the reason might be. Listen to these examples:

> Do you think he's found out about the customers' complaints?
> *Yes, he might have found out about that, I suppose.*
> Or could he have discovered that error in last month's accounts?
> *No, he can't have found out about that. I corrected it immediately.*

Now you go on in the same way. The notes will help you.

> Well, perhaps he's realized that you often arrive late.
> *Yes, he might have found out about that, I suppose.*
> Or maybe it's the fact that you've been borrowing from the petty cash?
> *No, he can't have found out about that. I paid it back last week.*
> Well, could it be those files you lost?
> *No, he can't have found out about that. I found them yesterday.*
> Well, what about the office window that got broken? Maybe it's that.
> *Yes, he might have found out about that, I suppose.*
> Or he may have heard that you always leave early in the evening?
> *No, he can't have found out about that. He always leaves before me.*
> I know, he's found out about all those phone calls you make to your friends.
> *Yes, he might have found out about that, I suppose.*

10  Could this have been prevented?

For the group work part of the step, roles could be assigned to each member of the group—solicitor, member of personnel department, project manager, member of the family, Fittenwell manager. The family and solicitor would insist on the fact that the company was negligent. The company representatives should explain that they did everything possible in the circumstances, and that local conditions meant they couldn't have dealt with the case any better. There is wide scope for invention of details on both sides, and the discussion will benefit from preparation either as homework or in class.

11 ✏️ Letter

Individual writing exercise for consolidation of language presented in the unit.

22 The new production plant

1 ▣ The information meeting (Tape section 51)

Listening and note-taking exercise. The tape should be played twice, at least, once for the information, then to determine how definite the following dates and plans are:

1	1st April	★ ★ ★
2	1st June	★
3	several new senior posts	
	one Swiss already appointed	★ ★ ★
	three to be advertised	★ ★ ★
	one internal appointment	★
	one or two seconded from Head Office	★ ★
	further appointments next year	★
4	workforce to be recruited from United Optics in Peterborough	★ ★
5	Marketing Department to remain here for the time being—will be expanded	★ ★ ★
6	only a handful of voluntary transfers	★ ★ ★
7	new sports and social centre to be completed before end of year	★ ★
8	housing problem in Peterborough—team investigating the situation	★ ★
9	five hundred units to be produced per month initially, then seven hundred and fifty	★ ★
10	insurance company may require alterations to the building	★

(★ ★ ★ indicates the most definite, ★ the least.)

2 ⌂ Decisions, plans, intentions

Ask the students to summarize orally the information they obtained from the tape. This will show what sections of the language summary to concentrate on.

3 ♟ Have you heard the latest?

One student introduces the rumour and another confirms or denies it, providing the correct information from the notes on the information meeting. In a competent class, all or part of the exercise could be done as pair work. More 'rumours' could be invented relating to Fittenwell or to the students' own jobs.

As a written exercise, this provides practice in expanding notes into complete sentences.

4 ⌂ Probability

Talking about the future, including conditional sentences. Examples for students' reference.

5 ✎ A gloomy outlook

Below are some model answers, but variations are of course possible.

1 *If the world economic recession continues, the number of unemployed is likely to increase.*
2 *There is some danger of inflation continuing to increase unless governments impose stricter monetary control.*
3 *Interest rates are sure to rise.*
4 *Gold prices might stabilize if there is no major world crisis.*
5 *The gulf separating North and South is unlikely to be reduced unless there is a considerable change in the world economic order.*
6 *There is very little chance of an alternative to nuclear power if the present low priority given to research continues.*

6 ♟ What do you think?

You may wish to introduce the activity by asking for ideas and writing some predictions on the board.

7 ▣ The minister's plans (Tape section 52)

Before listening to the tape, the class could predict how definite each of the projects 1 to 6 is, and write the press release (see below) using the expressions given. They then listen to the tape and make changes where necessary.

1 *There is a chance that we may begin construction of the Channel tunnel.*
2 *The Government's grant to local councils will be reduced.*
3 *We will be introducing measures to protect the countryside.*
4 *We are thinking of charging motorists a fee for using motorways.*

5 *We mean to set up a public enquiry into oil pollution on the Scottish coastline.*
6 *If the committee agrees, we will appoint a troubleshooter to investigate complaints from the public.*

8 ◯ Drill 1: There may be some delay... (*Tape section 53/1*)

Students respond with the help of the cuesheet in their books.

Tapescript:

You are talking to a visitor about plans for the new factory at Peterborough. She wants to know when they will be starting. Look at your cuesheet and listen to these examples.

So you've decided to redecorate the offices. When will work on that be starting?
Well, it should be starting next Monday, but there may be some delay.
And work on the new social centre—when will that be starting?
Well, it should be starting in June, but there may be some delay.

Now you go on in the same way. The cuesheet will give the dates you need.

And recruitment of new staff, when will you be holding interviews?
Well, they should be starting next Wednesday, but there may be some delay.
And the transfer of staff from Brighton to Peterborough, when will that start?
Well, it should be starting on the first of April, but there may be some delay.
And the advertising campaign for the new microscope—have you any dates for that?
Well, it should be starting at the beginning of May, but there may be some delay.
And what about production—when will that actually start.
Well, it should be starting in June, but there may be some delay.
And I believe you've been advised to overhaul the existing fire precautions. Have you started work on that yet?
Well, it should be starting on 15 April, but there may be some delay.
And I hear the electrical system needs some attention. Has that work been done yet?
Well, it should be starting on 10 April, but there may be some delay.
Well, I must say you don't sound too confident about the future!

◯ Drill 2: If they weren't so expensive... (*Tape section 53/2*)

Students respond with *Well we would... if it/they weren't so expensive.*

Tapescript:

Some of the office staff are complaining about working conditions and would like to see some changes made. You, however, are worried about costs. Listen to these examples:

The office typewriters are getting very unreliable. You should replace some of them.
Well, we would replace them if they weren't so expensive.
And the lighting is so poor. Why can't you install new lighting?
Well, we would install it if it weren't so expensive.

Now you go on in the same way.

And then there's the question of noise. Why don't you fit double glazing in the offices?
Well, we would fit it if it weren't so expensive.
And then there's the problem of getting to work. Couldn't the company organize transport for the staff?
Well, we would organize it if it weren't so expensive.
And the photocopier keeps breaking down. Why don't you buy a new one?
Well, we would buy a new one if it weren't so expensive.
And it gets so stuffy in the office. You really ought to put in air conditioning.
Well, we would put it in if it weren't so expensive.
And the overtime rate—it hasn't been increased for nearly three years.
Well, we would increase it if it weren't so expensive.
And we could do with a coffee machine in the office. Couldn't you hire one?
Well, we would hire one if it weren't so expensive.

9 Filming Fittenwell

Before dividing into groups, discuss what the interests of the four very different target audiences are. Point out that any which appear to interest all four groups should definitely be included in the film. In the case of a conflict of interests, which of the four groups is the most important? Draw attention to the limitations—time and money. A definite budget figure could be given. As the topic is a wide one, fix a time limit for the group discussion of approximately 20 minutes. Each group should make notes for the final class discussion.

23 Could I have your views?

1 📼 The meeting (1) *(Tape section 54)*

The first part of a three-stage meeting. Listening and note-taking exercise.
  Opinions expressed for and against are:
For: 1 *favourable financial, marketing and production reports;*
  2 *it's a worthwhile product;*
  3 *problems during trials have been ironed out.*
Against: 1 *it's too early to launch another new product;*
  2 *insufficient production capacity;*
  3 *there were set-backs during trials of the prototype.*

2 📖 Giving opinions

Remind students of exponents presented in previous units.

3 👥 The meeting (2)

The second stage of the meeting. Give students some time to prepare their roles. Encourage them to expand the notes and add further points. Their re-enactment of the meeting could be recorded.

📼 Play tape section 55 for comparison with the students' version. Discuss differences, concentrating on the opinion phrases heard on tape.

4 📖 Is it right for the job?

The use of certain intensifiers, laid out for students' reference.

5 ✏️ Just what we need . . . or is it?

Start with pair work. Then ask students to write a memo from the customer's purchasing assistant to his manager setting out the reasons for ordering or not ordering this machine.

6 📖 The chairman's role

Presentation of useful expressions for chairing a meeting.

7 👥 The meeting (3)

Free practice. Students could add more items to the *for* and *against* lists. No roles are necessary but discussion will be livelier if the group divides fairly evenly between those 'for' and 'against'.

8 🎧 Drill 1: True, but . . . *(Tape section 56/1)*

For controlled practice in expressing agreement. Students respond with *That may be true, but . . .*

Tapescript:

You disagree with your colleague's view that your products would be successful in Japan. Listen to these examples:

  Compared with the rest of Europe our prices are very competitive.
  That may be true, but they're not competitive enough for the Japanese market.
  And there's no doubt our methods are considered extremely efficient.
  That may be true, but they're not efficient enough for the Japanese market.

Now you go on in the same way.

  And our delivery periods are very short.
  That may be true, but they're not short enough for the Japanese market.
  Well, you must admit our product range is extremely wide.
  That may be true, but it's not wide enough for the Japanese market.
  Well, I'm sure you'll agree our payment terms are quite generous.
  That may be true, but they're not generous enough for the Japanese market.
  Well, the quality of our goods is higher than all our European competitors.
  That may be true, but it's not high enough for the Japanese market.

But you can't deny our designs are as good as any in the world.
That may be true, but they're not good enough for the Japanese market.
And we have a very satisfactory safety record.
That may be true, but it's not satisfactory enough for the Japanese market.

Drill 2: I'm afraid... *(Tape section 56/2)*

For controlled practice in a useful phrase for chairing meetings. Using notes in their books, students respond each time with *I'm afraid we must keep to the agenda. We're discussing..., not...*

Tapescript:

At a meeting of your department, colleagues find it difficult to keep to the point. You are the Chairman and you have to interrupt the speakers. Listen to these examples:

So he asked me what I thought of the new policy manual and I said...
I'm afraid we must keep to the agenda. We're discussing the training budget, not the policy manual.
And I've heard that there is to be a new Head of Personnel. Apparently he...
I'm afraid we must keep to the agenda. We're discussing staffing levels, not the Head of Personnel.

Now you go on in the same way. Look at the agenda in your book.

The men are really angry about the new work rota.
I'm afraid we must keep to the agenda. We're discussing overtime payments not the work rota.
And they were complaining the other day about the air conditioning.
I'm afraid we must keep to the agenda. We're discussing absenteeism, not the air conditioning.
And the boss wasn't too happy with the new budget, I can tell you. He said...
I'm afraid we must keep to the agenda. We're discussing the sales report, not the budget.
But I said we should first do something about the canteen food. I've never tasted anything...
I'm afraid we must keep to the agenda. We're discussing staff suggestions, not the canteen food.
And apparently he thinks the overtime payments are ridiculously low...
I'm afraid we must keep to the agenda. We're discussing the Middle East contract, not overtime payments.
So when he brought up the subject of annual holidays, I told him...
I'm afraid we must keep to the agenda. We're discussing the trade fair not annual holidays.

9 Innovation for industry

To promote livelier discussion individual members of the group could take the role of inventor of one of the ideas entered for the competition.

10 Report writing

The missing words, in order, are:

1 *the new X-ray equipment*
2 *put into production*
3 *confidence*
4 *doubts were expressed*
5 *production capacity*
6 *amount of research*
7 *it was agreed*
8 *in February*
9 *difference of opinion*
10 *manufacturing subsidiaries*
11 *some disagreement*
12 *it was finally decided*

24 Tell me why

1 Why have sales gone down? (Tape section 57)

Listening and note-taking exercise. The first part of a report.
  The reasons Paul Karim was given for the drop in sales are as follows.

Central London Hospital Purchasing Officer:
  budget cut;
  unreliable delivery dates;
  increase in prices.
British Doctors' Council:
  high prices;
  side-effects of vinacyn;
  new Medax analgesic.
Ministry of Health:
  trade deficit;
  expansion of National Pharmaceutical Company;
  anxiety about dangerous drugs.

2 Asking for reasons

Useful phrases for asking for (and giving) reasons, for students' reference.

3 This is the reason

Play the first part of the report again (tape section 57) for students to note down which reason is the main one. The sentences could be written at home:

1 *BDC have reduced their orders chiefly because of the side-effects of vinacyn, but our high prices and competition from Medax may have been contributory factors.*
2 *Orders from CLH have gone down chiefly because of the increase in prices but the cut in their budget and our unreliable delivery dates may have been contributory factors.*
3 *The Ministry of Health have ordered less chiefly because of their anxiety about dangerous drugs, but their trade deficit and the expansion of their own pharmaceutical company may have been contributory factors.*

4 All is not lost (Tape section 58)

Second part of the report. Students could work in groups of three, one noting the positive comments, another the alternative sources and the third the recommendations. Each group would then exchange their information. Play the tape a second time as a check.

5 Connectors

Presentation of useful words and phrases for connecting and contrasting statements.

6 Positive thinking

The summary of the report could be prepared orally, then written up for homework.

7 The tax office

Give students some time to read the problem— a homework exercise possibly. Fix a time limit for the group discussion. Appoint one person from each group to take notes and read out the group's conclusions.

8 Drill 1: Mainly due to . . . (Tape section 59/1)

Controlled practice in presenting main and supplementary reasons. Students respond with two reasons, using the notes in their books. *Reason (1)* is the main reason (*. . . mainly due to . . .*); *Reason (2)* is the supplementary reason (*. . . might have had something to do with it.*). The drill proper starts with 'Italy'.

Tapescript:

You are Export Sales Manager. Generally, results for the last twelve months were less good than the previous year. Use the cuesheet in your book to explain last year's results. Listen to these examples:

  Now then, Smith, apart from a couple of areas, results this year have been pretty poor, wouldn't you agree?

Well, the decline in sales in France was mainly due to competition from Italy, but anti-British feeling might have had something to do with it.
But in Germany we seem to have done quite well—why is this?
Well, the increase in sales in Germany was mainly due to the favourable exchange rate, but last year's advertising campaign might have had something to do with it.

Now, using the notes, go on in the same way.

And in Italy too, we've been quite successful I see.
Well, the increase in sales in Italy was mainly due to the devaluation of the lira, but our excellent new agent might have had something to do with it.
But there's been a real slump in Japan.
Well, the decline in sales in Japan was mainly due to the difficulty in obtaining import licences, but the language barrier might have had something to do with it.
And Scandinavia—I'm most surprised at the poor results there.
Well, the decline in sales in Scandinavia was mainly due to illness amongst our sales staff, but the strength of the pound might have had something to do with it.
The situation in Spain looks a little better.
Well, the increase in sales in Spain was mainly due to two government contracts, but our reputation for quality products might have had something to do with it.
And whatever happened in North Africa? You were so optimistic last year.
Well, the decline in sales in North Africa was mainly due to the unsettled political situation, but the arrest of our local agent might have had something to do with it.
And the USA—those figures make gloomy reading. We'd expected a better showing.
Well, the decline in sales in the USA was mainly due to the general economic recession, but our poor after-sales service might have had something to do with it.
Well, you seem to have an explanation for everything—how about coming up with some remedies!

Drill 2: An exciting life (*Tape section 59/2*)

For controlled practice in connecting sentences, using these phrases: *Yes . . . and what is more . . .*; *Yes, but although . . .*; *Yes . . . and consequently . . . .* A good class will know which connecting phrases to use from the two notes provided for each response. A weaker class may need a fuller introduction.

Tapescript:

Listen to Natasha Kydd, a well-known journalist being interviewed about her job.

I suppose most people would consider your life a very exciting one.
Yes, it is very exciting and what is more it is very well paid.
And the people you meet—some of them are very wealthy.
Yes, but although they are very wealthy, they are not usually very happy.
I see. Are you sometimes in dangerous situations?
Yes, I am sometimes in dangerous situations and consequently I always carry a gun.

Now you go on in the same way. The interviewer's notes will help you. You are Natasha.

And have you ever used your gun?
Yes, but although I have used it, I've never killed anyone.
I'm glad to hear it! Er, you were telling me that you were very nervous when you interviewed the President last week, so nervous that your hands were shaking.
Yes, my hands were shaking and consequently I dropped my tape recorder.
Was the President startled?
Yes, but although he was startled he continued talking quite calmly.
I've heard that you pilot your own helicopter?
Yes, I pilot my own helicopter and what is more I drive racing cars.
You once said that you would leave journalism to write novels if you had enough money. You are now very rich I believe.
Yes, I am very rich and consequently I am giving up my job at the end of the year.
Well, I wish you every success in the world.

9 Musicbox plays a sad song

Reading and note-taking exercise.

1 *False*   5 *True*
2 *False*   6 *True*
3 *True*   7 *False*
4 *False*   8 *False*

10 How do you explain it?

Directors could take roles—financial director, marketing, production, planning and so on. Shareholders should insist on full and satisfactory explanations and positive action for the future.

11 Report writing

Students write individual reports on the meeting, possibly for homework.

25 That's the way it is

1 ▭ It's not allowed—or is it? (*Tape section 60*)

Listening and note-taking exercise. *TV commercials, cure, refund*, may need to be explained.

1 Adverts in medical journals: *permitted*
2 TV commercials: *restricted*
3 Cure claims: *prohibited*
4 Doctor's recommendation: *restricted*
5 Refund offer: *prohibited*

2 ☞ Is it allowed?

Language summary. This could be followed by a discussion of advertising standards in the students' countries.

3 ✎ Advertising standards

Insist on students using the forms presented in step 2, not simply reading the printed extracts. Point out the frequent use of *should* in written rules and regulations. Students should write sentences like the following:

1 *You can only offer credit if you give the name and address of the advertiser.*
2 *Off-shore radio stations are forbidden.*
3 *You are not allowed to use the Red Cross or Red Crescent in advertisements.*
4 *You can only advertise the owner, charterer or manufacturer on aircraft.*
5 *Children mustn't appear in advertisements doing dangerous things.*
6 *It is absolutely forbidden to encourage law-breaking.*
7 *You're not allowed to have children in a scene with an open fire unless there is a fireguard.*

4 ♟ Diplomat King Size

This could be a straightforward exercise with students making one sentence about each proposal using the language forms presented, or a freer group discussion. Information on the advertising budget, target market, etc, could be invented before deciding what form the campaign should take.

5 ▭ I told you so (*Tape section 61*)

Listening comprehension. Introduce the topic of international tenders. Refer to invitations to tender in English language newspapers, if available.

1 False   6 True
2 True   7 True
3 True   8 True
4 True   9 False
5 False

6 ☞ Regrets and recriminations

Presentation of examples. Ask students to make up other sentences.

7 ✎ Problems of an advertising agency

Students write sentences with *I wish* and *if only*. Prepare orally, and point out the different tenses these two phrases take, before asking students to write sentences like the following:

1 *I wish we hadn't lost the Ambermold contract.*
2 *If only IGM would renew their contract with us.*
3 *I wish he hadn't left.*
4 *If only they weren't cutting their budgets.*
5 *If only they weren't putting up the TV rates.*
6 *I wish she would stop complaining.*
7 *I wish we could afford to move to bigger offices.*
8 *If only Global Motors would give us more time.*

8 ♫ Drill 1: Yes or no? (*Tape section 62/1*)

Using the notes in their books, students respond with *Yes, you can . . . provided that . . .* (*must* in the notes) or *No, it's absolutely forbidden . . .* or *Well, you're not supposed to . . .* (*not officially allowed* in the notes).
  Note: there are two possible responses, using either the pronoun (for example 'it') or the noun (for example 'the camera').

Tapescript:

Before going on a marketing trip to Eastern Europe,

Mr Grayson is enquiring about regulations that apply to visiting businessmen. Look at the notes in your book and listen to these examples:

Now first of all, are you allowed to import a typewriter? I always like to type my own reports.
Yes, you can import a typewriter provided that you declare it to the customs authorities.
Right, then a friend of mind gave me about £20 worth of the local currency, but I'm not sure if you're allowed to bring it into the country.
No, it's absolutely forbidden to bring local currency into the country.
OK. Then, when I'm there, I've heard they like to deal with all foreign trade through a central organization. Now, does this mean I can't contact individual companies?
Well, you're not supposed to contact individual companies.

Now you go on. Use the notes to give the information required.

Then there's my camera—photography's my hobby you know—I can take it with me, can't I?
Yes, you can take it with you provided you declare it to the customs authorities.
And what about actually taking photos. Can I take photos anywhere I like?
No, it's absolutely forbidden to take photos near military areas.
Right, I'll be careful of that. And another thing, I hear people often offer to change money for you, in the hotel or in the street. Are you allowed to change foreign currency like that?
No, it's absolutely forbidden to change foreign currency with private individuals.
I see, now I'm not sure where I'll be staying. I've heard it's possible to have my letters sent care of the British Embassy.
Yes, you can have them sent care of the British Embassy provided you let them know in advance.
And I believe you're not allowed to import any foreign newspapers, is that right?
Well, you're not supposed to import any foreign newspapers . . .
I see, just as long as they don't find them . . . !

◯ Drill 2: It wouldn't have happened if . . . *(Tape section 62/2)*

Students use the notes to respond with conditional sentences.

Tapescript:

A colleague of yours is talking about various problems in the company. You feel that these could have been avoided. Listen to these examples:

Management—labour relations are really bad at the moment.
They wouldn't be bad if the Union Representative hadn't been sacked last month.
And productivity dropped by 15% last month.
It wouldn't have dropped if there hadn't been a 'flu epidemic.

Notice that if the problem is now you use *would* or *wouldn't* and the infinitive: *They wouldn't be bad*. And if the problem was in the past you use *would have* or *wouldn't have* and the past participle: *It wouldn't have dropped*. Now you respond in the same way, using the notes in your book.

And Browning from Export Sales says their orders are very low.
They wouldn't be low if we had spent enough money on promotions abroad.
Yes, that's probably true. And then there's the clerical staff. They're very discontented at the moment.
They wouldn't be discontented if Management had given them a pay rise.
Yes, but money is really tight. Apparently there's a serious cash flow problem this year.
There wouldn't be a cash flow problem if the bank had extended their loan.
True. I think the bank has certainly not been very helpful. And the shareholders aren't happy. Their dividend was very low last year.
It wouldn't have been low if we had made a high enough profit.
Of course, and we would have, if we'd won the Japanese contract—but there you are, we didn't!
We would have won the Japanese contract if our delivery date had been early enough.
Yes, we've really got to be more competitive.
We would be more competitive if the Board of Directors had adopted the working party's proposals.
You could well be right. Well, I suppose it's time for lunch now . . .

9 ☺ Why did it go wrong?

When the problem has been discussed in small groups and decisions have been taken regarding future campaigns, each group's conclusions could be compared and the differences discussed.

10 ✎ A strongly worded letter

Individual writing practice. Students should use the phrases and constructions introduced in step 6.

26 Keep the customer satisfied

This unit differs in that it consists of a problem-solving exercise with a variety of input. It gives an opportunity to revise the skills, structures and functions practised in previous units.

1 📼 Can we do it? *(Tape section 63)*

Listening and note-taking exercise. Revision points could be future arrangements and plans, requests and dates.

1. JX Imports, Jeddah: *12–15 May*
    Hospital Supplies, Johannesburg: *15–21 May*
    Medicaid, London: *30 May*
    Central State Hospital, Montreal: *14–17 May*
    HMB, Buenos Aires: *10–14 May*
2. Peter Rittman: *1–15 May*
    Claud Harz: *15–30 May*
3. Peter Rittman will be on holiday.
    Claud Harz's wife is expecting a baby.

2 👥 The best we can do (1)

Revision of suggesting, agreeing and disagreeing. The best time schedule will probably be:

P Rittman:
1. *Jeddah: 16–20 May*
2. *Johannesburg: 20–27 May*

C Harz:
1. *Buenos Aires: 7–11 May*
2. *Montreal: 11–14 May*
3. *London: 31 May*

3 👆 The gerund

Presentation, for students' reference, of some gerund (and infinitive) constructions.

4 ✏️ Letter to a friend

Written practice of gerund and infinitive constructions. Answers are:

(1) *to get*   (6) *saying*   (11) *feeling*
(2) *to disturb* (7) *take*   (12) *working*
(3) *to be*   (8) *consulting* (13) *taking*
(4) *wasting*   (9) *spending*   (14) *complaining*
(5) *attending*   (10) *attending* (15) *to tell*
(16) *finding*   (18) *hearing*   (20) *to know*
(17) *sailing*   (19) *asking*   (21) *hearing*

5 📼 Complications *(Tape section 64)*

Listening and note-taking exercise.
The details to be noted down during steps 5 and 6 are as follows:

CSH, Montreal: *Inspection 18 May. Strike 10–13 May. Must come on dates requested.*
Karim, Jeddah: *Religious festival 16–23 May. MD in Europe until 10 May.*
HS, Johannesburg: *Insist on original dates. Threaten to change suppliers.*

6 👥 More trouble

One student in each pair reads the letter, the other the telex. Encourage them to use reported speech in their exchange of information (see above).

7 📼 Worse to come *(Tape section 65)*

Short note-taking and listening exercise.

8 🎧 Drill 1: There's absolutely no question . . . *(Tape section 66/1)*

Controlled practice in the use of the gerund.

Tapescript:

Rumours are circulating about drastic cuts being made in the company. You give very positive reassurance to the Trade Union representative. Listen to these examples:

We're all extremely worried, Mr Brown. There are rumours that you're planning to make 200 redundant.
No, there's absolutely no question of making 200 redundant.
And it's said our goods are too expensive. We've heard you intend to use lower quality materials.
No, there's absolutely no question of using lower quality materials.

Now you go on in the same way.

> Another thing. It is true that you are going to cut salaries?
> *No, there's absolutely no question of cutting salaries.*
> Well, what about working hours? Rumour has it you're going to increase working hours.
> *No, there's absolutely no question of increasing working hours.*
> And they also say you intend to reduce overtime payments.
> *No, there's absolutely no question of reducing overtime payments.*
> I've also heard you mean to phase out our after-sales service.
> *No, there's absolutely no question of phasing out our after-sales service.*
> And they're saying in Personnel that you want to stop the staff training programme.
> *No, there's absolutely no question of stopping the staff training programme.*
> And what about prices in the canteen? Do you intend to charge more in the staff canteen?
> *No, there's absolutely no question of charging more in the staff canteen.*

Drill 2: There's no alternative...
(*Tape section 66/2*)

For controlled practice in the use of an infinitive construction.

Tapescript:

You are due to leave this afternoon on a business trip, visiting Frankfurt, then Berlin. You have just heard that bad weather has closed down Frankfurt airport. Listen to these examples:

> I'm afraid your trip to Frankfurt will have to be postponed.
> *Yes, it seems there's no alternative but to postpone my trip to Frankfurt.*
> And the meeting this evening will have to be cancelled.
> *Yes, it seems there's no alternative but to cancel the meeting this evening.*

Now you go on in the same way:

> So the rest of your trip will have to be rescheduled.
> *Yes, it seems there's no alternative but to reschedule the rest of my trip.*
> So your flight reservation will have to be changed.
> *Yes, it seems there's no alternative but to change my flight reservation.*
> Your visit to Berlin will have to be brought forward.
> *Yes, it seems there's no alternative but to bring forward my visit to Berlin.*
> That means your hotel booking will have to be altered.
> *Yes, it seems there's no alternative but to alter my hotel booking.*
> And your hotel room in Frankfurt will have to be cancelled.
> *Yes, it seems there's no alternative but to cancel my hotel room in Frankfurt.*
> A telex explaining the situation will have to be sent.
> *Yes, it seems there's no alternative but to send a telex explaining the situation.*

9 The best we can do (2) (*Tape section 67*)

Listening and note-taking exercise. Students should summarize all the information they now have in note form.

All the factors should be borne in mind (see below). It may be necessary to work out whether one client is more important than another, and which seems most likely to create trouble for the company if their demands are not met.

10. We are pleased to be able to tell you...

Present these phrases, and any others you think may be useful, before students start written consolidation.

Client	Dates requested	Engineers' availability	Other factors
J X Imports, Jeddah	12–15 May	Either 16–31 or 1–17 May	Religious holiday 16–23. Managing Director away until 10 May.
HS, Johannesburg	15–21 May	1–17 May	Very insistant on keeping to original dates.
HMB, Buenos Aires	10–14 May	1–19 May	—
CSH, Montreal	14–17 May	1–19 May	Staff strike 10–13 May. Inspection 18 May.
Medicaid, London	30 May	1–19 May	Airport strike 30 May–5 June.

27 Consolidation exercises

The language points tested are those covered in Units 19 to 26. Exercise 3 tests *didn't need to* and *needn't have* which has not been treated as a separate language point but can be expected to come up in Unit 21. The key gives model answers to open-ended questions.

Extra role plays and discussions could be built round exercise 5 (whether to set up an electro-plating factory in South America) and exercises 1 and 2 (sales visit to Scotland).

KEY

1 Requests and offers

1 Will you find out about flight and accommodation?
2 I'd be grateful if you could provide information about relevant tax laws.
3 Could you tell me the time, please?
4 Do you think I could possibly move to a quieter room?
5 I wonder if you could give me a receipt.

1 We could offer a discount of 12½% on the list price.
2 We could train the operators, should you wish it, and at no extra charge.
3 We'll tailor the design to your exact specifications, if you like.
4 We could always send an engineer to supervise the installation.
5 Would you like to come to dinner this evening?

2 A big future

Paragraph 1:
(1) opportunities
(2) skilled
(3) grants
(4) investment
(5) legislation
(6) repatriated

Paragraph 2:
(7) decline
(8) boom
(9) exploited
(10) provide
(11) sector

3 Needn't have . . .

I didn't need to distribute fact sheets about the chemical processes involved.
I needn't have explained the history of our company.
I needn't have given details of our new machine.
I needn't have talked about R and D.
I didn't need to tell them about the situation in the United States.
I didn't need to show them our film.
I needn't have outlined the latest research in the field.
I needn't have visited the Polytechnic.

4 A decline in sales

The reasons for the decline in sales of our electro-plating equipment are complex. Perhaps the most important change in the past few years has been the increased availability of cheap imports, particularly from Korea and Taiwan. Given the fact that there has been an overall fall in the amount of electro-plating world-wide as well, the results have been disastrous for our company. A contributory reason could well be that there have been reliability problems with some of our machines, and more than one customer has complained about long delivery periods. This has not been helped at all by the high value of our domestic currency. One final reason which has been put forward to explain the present situation is our low rates of commission to agents. So, all in all, the outlook is rather bleak in our line of business.

5 Allowed, prohibited, restricted

You are allowed to import parts for assembly as long as you inform the Ministry of Industry.
You can repatriate profits provided you pay 10% local tax.
You are not allowed to use the factory 24 hours a day, 7 days a week.
You can employ Europeans as supervisors and engineers as long as 20% are local people.
You are allowed to use dangerous chemicals in the production process as long as the workers have protective clothing.
You are permitted to take over local companies provided